PARANORMAL
CAMBRIDGESHIRE

PARANORMAL
CAMBRIDGESHIRE

DAMIEN O'DELL

AMBERLEY

First published 2011

Amberley Publishing
The Hill, Stroud
Gloucestershire, GL5 4EP

www.amberleybooks.com

British Library Cataloguing in Publication Data.
A catalogue record for this book is available from the British Library.

ISBN 978 1 84868 138 5

Typesetting and Origination by Amberley Publishing.
Printed in Great Britain.

Contents

A ghostly lady. A genuine ghost or merely double exposure? This photograph was taken many years ago and was to be used in a series of Cambridge postcards. The photographer was certain that it was not a double exposure. He was equally convinced that no-one had been standing in front of the door when he took the picture. He maintained that he had captured a ghost on film.

CHAPTER ONE

Marshall's Manifestations

During 1998/99, I was earning a comfortable living as a successful fork truck sales engineer, working for the world's largest fork truck manufacturers, Lansing Linde, when I clinched a very big deal at a company called Marshall's Aerospace, based at Cambridge Airport, on the south side of the Newmarket Road. Marshall's was a company with an international reputation. I will never forget my first visit to the site, an enormous engineering works spread over many acres. There were numerous hangers where aircraft were serviced and modified, it ran 'twenty-four seven' and business was brisk. Marshall's Aerospace was a particularly impressive concern because it was only a part of a much larger conglomerate, which is still run by the Marshall family. They even had their own company fire service at the airfield.

On the other side of the Newmarket Road (north side) was the Garage Group, which held franchises to sell new Rover and Jaguar motor cars, and there was a thriving second-hand car business here too. These premises extended from the cemetery to Teversham Corner Garage and Thermos King. Behind that was Marshall Specialist Vehicles, where I saw British Army vehicles being adapted for various different uses as were Post Office vans, passenger buses, etc. In December 1998 I clinched a deal with David Bianco, then Marshall's Chief Buyer, for five 3-ton H30D diesel forklift trucks. This was only the start of the business to come, which was to be my largest-ever order from the Cambridgeshire patch. The total amount of materials handling equipment business from Marshall's ran well into six figures.

While I was producing record sales with Marshall's, stories of multiple haunting at the airport site were filtering out, which I avidly collected. Unbeknownst to me, an employee at the company, David Curry, a security officer, was doing his own on-site research, which culminated in his book, *The Men That Never Clocked Off*, which he self-published in 2004. My own enquiries tallied with David's, although we had not met then and were working independently, each unaware of the other's interest. Whereas David worked alone as a ghost hunter I went on to form my own paranormal investigation group, APIS (Anglia Paranormal Investigation Society).

THE ADMINISTRATION BLOCK

Undoubtedly the most haunted part of the Marshall's complex is the Administration Block, which was built in 1938. Cleaners and security men regularly reported odd occurrences in this building. One of the strangest reported incidents was made by a cleaner, who was working one Sunday while her son sat and listened to his cassette radio. The machine suddenly stopped working and as it did so the boy heard footsteps walking down the passage towards the air traffic area and the tower. He noticed that his watch had stopped working also. This is a common phenomenon that I've witnessed many times at haunted locations. When 'battery drain' occurs, fully charged batteries in cameras, watches, torches and other electrical items go flat in seconds. One theory is that whatever is responsible for the haunting drains any available electrical source and utilises that energy to create paranormal effects. That same afternoon, as the boy's mother sat in the same room reading the newspaper before resuming work, she too heard footsteps coming from the same direction as heard by her son earlier on. She opened the door and realised that the passageway door hadn't opened as the 'person' passed by and there was nobody to be seen now.

Footsteps passing overhead were reported by another cleaner in the same area some years later. Once again the building was empty. This was confirmed by a

The Admin Block. Phenomena reported here include the apparitions of an RAF officer and former office workers, the smell of pipe tobacco and the sounds of phantom footsteps.

security man who had a similar experience while on duty and alone in the Admin Block. A fifth witness was on night shift and in Admin to do some photocopying; as he left he, too, heard footsteps above him in the passageway. Once outside he looked up but there was no sign of life, not even a flashlight to account for any presence on the floor above. Yet another witness, while on security duty, heard footsteps on the wooden stairs leading to the main conference room, footsteps that never reached the bottom …

At the north end of the Admin Block, on the ground floor, the Air Cadets had offices, until they moved out in 1999. There was an Officer-in-Charge (OC) office, a television room and rest rooms for the aircrews. A lady who had been a cleaner here for many years was walking toward these offices when she saw an RAF officer come in from the street and walk towards the OC's office. He was wearing blue trousers and a blue jumper. When the cleaner reached the office she found the door closed, so she knocked on it but it was locked. Using a pass key she entered the office – only to find it empty. The next day, as this same lady was cleaning the crew room, she became aware of someone standing next to her wearing black shoes and blue trousers, but as she looked up to see the rest of the figure it disappeared. Before this sighting another Marshall employee, who had been working on his own in the passageway, had seen a man in full Second World War flying clothes going into the Officer-in-Charge's office …

The parachute store was where Air Cadets would put on their 'chutes preparatory to their first flight. A highly experienced security man was on duty one Saturday night in March 1999 when he repeatedly heard the door to the store banging. This had never happened before, but each time he checked the room the banging would stop. He brought along a colleague to investigate but there were no windows open and the store's door was covered with racking containing the cadets' helmets, so there was no reason for this particular door to bang. Later on it was found that a parachute room worker with many years' service had died two years previously … in March.

A man who worked for most of his life in the parachute packing room heard the sound of a young girl's voice singing on one occasion when he was alone. He looked up in the direction of the sound to the area known as 'the loft', where, to his surprise, he saw a young girl standing there singing softly. The next moment she simply vanished.

In his book, *The Men That Never Clocked Off*, security man David Curry admitted to feeling a presence in the Air Cadets' offices and he was probably a lot more psychically sensitive then than he realised. He felt pins and needles on his back and legs as he unlocked the outer door leading to the rest room and when he unlocked the inner door the pins and needles increased. He discovered that talking to the 'presence' made the pins and needles go away. When he reached a large armchair by the sink the pins and needles would return, but with increased intensity. This was a regular occurrence that Curry interpreted as the ghost's way of letting him know that it was around. The security man noted the fact that the end of the month was the time when the 'presence' was most strongly felt, as with the other manifestations at Marshall's. He was particularly pleased when he had someone to corroborate his paranormal experiences, as happened on an early evening in November 2003. While on patrol David smelt the sweet smell of pipe tobacco in the Administration Block reception area. He had noticed this aroma at various times of the day and night, usually when the place was unoccupied. He went upstairs to fetch a cleaner who, on coming downstairs to establish if she could smell anything, unhesitatingly volunteered that she could plainly smell pipe tobacco in this non-smoking building.

A cleaning supervisor found two of her girls 'in a terrible state' one August evening after they had experienced a frightening encounter. The cleaners had been having a coffee break at around 8 p.m. when they heard loud footsteps approaching them on the parquet flooring from the direction of the wages department. Nearer and nearer the sounds came until reaching a set of wooden fire doors, just a matter of feet away from the startled women. The fire doors opened with a squeak before closing again, and then all went quiet. The pair got up and in the time it would have taken for someone to walk to the next set of fire doors these doors opened and closed, also by themselves yet the footsteps resumed on the other side of them. Now badly frightened, the girls rushed to open the doors to get a good view ... of a straight, empty corridor. Two years afterwards one of the same ladies was with a new cleaner and the pair had finished their work and were waiting to go home. They sat together, chatting in one of the offices, when they suddenly heard a heavy tread coming up the wooden stairs, the fire door on the landing opened and closed, heavy footsteps continued to the coffee vending machines, and then stopped. The ladies got up and went out to the landing but there was no trace of anybody about.

There was an increase in paranormal events, as is so often the case, after the Administration Block underwent major modernisation, renovation and repainting work in 2001. A young girl who worked in quality control felt, on several occasions, a strong sensation of someone standing behind her as she sat at her desk. When he was on night duty, David Curry made a point of investigating this particular office. Making sure that he was alone he locked the doors and sat without any lights on behind the girl's desk. After about half an hour, once his eyes had adjusted to the low light, he got up and stopped to get a good view across the long room. As he looked at a door with a small glass pane in it he distinctly saw a man move across the door before suddenly disappearing. There was no detail, no face or even arms or legs moving, just an all-black impression of a man of around average height. When Curry discussed his sighting with the office staff, a serious, well-educated young man came forward, who was not given to 'telling tales' and admitted to seeing an apparition in this same office during the daytime. It was soon after 7 a.m. one morning and he was sitting at his desk when he looked up to see the head and shoulders of a man walking across the other side of the office. The weird thing was that he could see through him – the 'visitor' was transparent!

David Curry, fascinated by the reports coming from the haunted Quality Control Office, decided to do some more 'psychic sleuthing' and one night, as he was searching for 'cold spots', the outside telephone rang, then it stopped and the internal phone began to ring. Thinking that he had been the victim of pranksters, Curry checked with his security colleagues, only to discover that at least one of them had had an identical experience. Office staff confirmed that no-one would have any reason to call these numbers out of hours. In fact, the office manager had witnessed an even more peculiar occurrence one afternoon when he saw his wedding photo rise about a foot off his desk before flipping over backwards and throwing itself onto the floor in front of his desk. This event was also witnessed by an amazed female colleague, with whom he had been talking.

David Curry was later interviewed by a reporter from the *Cambridge News*. 'My interest in the airport's ghosts started way back in 1977, when I began working there. People told me there had been all sorts of sightings over the years and of course I took it with a pinch of salt. Being a new boy I was fair game for such things. Then I met Phyllis Whitley, an office cleaner, and she was full of stories about ghosts, not just walking around the offices and workshops but outside on the airfield itself.' Any scepticism that David still harboured was soon blown away in the face of personal experience. He said, 'I was sitting in the Airport Drawing Office one night at Christmas time, a big open-plan office and I clearly heard someone say something – I'm not sure what it was but there was no-one there. The way I investigate a ghost report is firstly to look at the person telling the story. Can I be sure they are telling me the truth? If I know them it is easy, if not then I have to go and ask those who work alongside them and then go by what they say and my own gut instincts. I then look at the place where the event happened. Have I had other reports from the same area? If so are they the same? Can I eliminate any noise or movement that could be mistaken for a ghost? Lighting can play a big part in some sightings. I've spent many a night walking around the airport works hoping to see or hear a ghost then when I'm least expecting it, it happens. Sometimes I feel scared but not all of the time. I've racked my brains to work out why there should have been so many ghostly sightings at the airport and all I can think of is that so many people have worked there over so long a time that they have left a kind of imprint on the place – they have physically gone but they have never really clocked off.'

THE HANGARS

Although the Admin Block was the focus of numerous paranormal phenomena, the hangars also featured heavily in reports of a similar nature. Many episodes occurred on a Saturday, one such was recorded in Hangar Four, which was known as T2 and it had been in operation during the Second World War for aircraft repairs and maintenance. This was to be the best authenticated sighting in the haunted history of Marshall's Aerospace. On this particular night in 1958, at one o'clock in the morning, an eight-man maintenance crew were having a meal break. The men were working through the night on a Canberra aircraft and needed refreshment. They settled down to chat about football, holidays and other interests while they drank their tea and ate their sandwiches. Suddenly one of them looked towards the end of the hanger and froze. 'Who the bloody hell is that at this time of night?' he asked his workmates. Walking towards them was a pilot in full wartime kit: flying boots, fur-lined flying jacket, helmet and goggles. The night shift sat there open mouthed as the figure approached, then turned and went into a locked office. The maintenance crew rushed in a body to the place where the airman had gone. One of them unlocked the office, only to find it empty. There was no other possible exit and the realisation dawned on them that they had seen a ghost. This incident caused quite a stir at the time as it was witnessed by so many employees. Later on this area became the paint shop for army lorries and many accounts of tools being thrown on the floor by invisible forces, particularly during meal breaks, were received. One unfortunate paint sprayer had his airline snatched from under his arm by an unseen presence on more than one occasion. The restroom, which was formerly an air-raid shelter on the side of this hangar, was not immune to unexplained incidents. Preparatory to a 'brew up', one of the lads had put the kettle on to boil and set up some mugs for his workmates. Upon his return all the mugs had been turned upside down yet he was sure that nobody had been into the restroom in his brief absence and this was not an isolated incident, it was repeated on at least one other occasion …

A security guard had a narrow escape when alone in one of the hangars on another Saturday; this time it was in the afternoon. He nearly jumped out of his skin when there was an almighty crash close by as he was passing the tailplane of a giant C-130 aircraft. An iron bar, about 4 feet long and weighing some 20 pounds, had fallen from the staging surrounding the plane. He craned his neck upwards but there was nobody up there who could have knocked the bar off the staging. Another guard was patrolling at night in Number Two Hangar when his attention was arrested by the sight of a man walking through solid work benches … then the apparition just faded away.

At least one ghost was named and it was Mac Hale, a deceased employee who had worked at Marshall's for some thirty years, from the 1940s till his retirement in 1974. David Curry was puzzled by the strange sounds that distracted him from his book in the wee small hours of a Sunday morning security shift in Hangar Two, reputedly the most haunted building at the airport. First he heard footsteps crossing an empty shop floor then whistling. In David Curry's own words, 'a toneless tune and shuffling his feet as he moved slowly towards the centre of the hangar'. Although Curry could clearly hear 'something' there was nothing to be seen. The security guard was later told by an older member of the workforce that this was definitely characteristic of Mac Hale. This long-serving employee in later years had bad feet and a chest problem that caused him to whistle tunelessly.

Poltergeist activity was reported from Hangar Thirteen with the sudden disappearance of a tape measure that had been just put down. The workman involved in this incident was not too worried because he had a spare tape in his bag a short distance away. Upon opening his bag he was amazed to find two tapes. His spare one was there plus the one that had so mysteriously and suddenly disappeared.

An overhead crane's control box was found wildly swinging around with nobody nearby on another occasion. Other anomalous phenomena witnessed in Hangar Thirteen included the sudden, unaccountable smell of perfume, strange cold draughts, a 'black shape' seen moving about and whispering was heard.

During a shift one Christmas, Curry had a brush with a ghost in Hangar Ten. It was around 11 p.m. when the security man looked up to see a man watching him from the glass office block. The man was wearing a suit from the 1940s/50s with collar and tie. He was in his sixties with short hair and was clean-shaven. Another ex-employee who never clocked off?

Sometimes it was the aircraft that were haunted, bringing their own invisible passengers with them. On a Tri-star L101 jet, which was in for a service, sounds of someone walking around the passenger deck were clearly heard by a fitter one night as he was working alone in the cargo bay. The fitter told a colleague and together they searched the plane only to find it devoid of any human occupation but themselves.

Hangar Three was used as a garage but had earlier seen service for aircraft repairs. It was the scene of an extremely rare occurrence in the world of the paranormal: an aircraft fitter had a conversation with a ghost! The mechanic was working on an Airspeed Oxford when he looked up to see an RAF officer in front of him. The RAF man asked for the location of an aircraft that was in for repair and even quoted its identification number. The fitter gave directions and moved out of sight around the corner. Another fitter appeared around the same corner shortly afterwards and the first fitter enquired if he had seen the RAF man as he must have passed him. The new arrival denied seeing any such person so the two fitters set off in search of the mystery man. They checked with the entire night shift but nobody else had seen the stranger. This building was pulled down in the late

1990s to make way for the new car centre, as Marshall's had gained the franchise to sell the latest range of Rovers.

THE MACHINE SHOP

Interactive ghosts are rare enough but ghosts that communicate are much rarer still – which makes the following stories so interesting. Machine Shop 1, like so many of the buildings at Marshall's, has undergone several changes of use over the years. It was used by airmen in the Second World War, then after the war it became a milling and grinding shop. Finally, it closed in 2001 to become a garage workshop. It became known as the haunt of 'the Grey Man'. The reputation was confirmed when a cleaner on a tea break looked up from his newspaper to see before him, framed in the doorway, a complete stranger – a well-dressed man with a very grey looking face. The startled cleaner automatically asked if everything was all right, and the grey man replied 'Yes' before disappearing. The cleaner was quickly on his feet to discover what had become of the unexpected visitor, but could find no sign of him. Even odder, on questioning his workmates nobody else had either seen the smartly suited man come or go in the building. Many years before, during the war, Marshall's were hard at work turning aircraft into tankers for the RAF so that they could be flown south with much needed supplies to fight the war. It was around midnight and a workman was making aircraft parts when a cold shudder ran down his back and he felt compelled to turn around. Not ten feet away stood a strange man in a suit. This time the suited man asked 'Is everything all right?' The worker replied that it was and bent down to his task again, when he looked up there was no sign of his unexpected visitor. He left his workbench to search for the man but the Machine Shop was deserted.

MACHINE SHOP 2

The store above the nightshift office in the workshop was a place with a well-deserved reputation for being haunted. Four workers were on their tea break, at about 1 a.m., when they distinctly heard footsteps on the wooden floor overhead. An enthusiastic search was made but the storeroom was found to be empty. During the coming months, the sounds were heard on a number of occasions, at various times and days; sometimes the footsteps were heard ascending the stairs as well. In time the unexplained footsteps were accepted and nobody bothered to search the empty store. One of the workmen had a bad fright one night when he nipped up to the store for forty winks during the tea break. Finding a comfortable corner with some soft covers on the floor he was soon fast asleep, but when he woke up he was freezing cold, which was strange because it was a hot summer's night. As he sat up he could see that he was no longer alone. Someone was standing watching him and in the darkened room he could make out a figure wearing a peaked cap, with a shiny belt buckle and some kind of uniform. He rushed out of the room and told his workmates. They duly checked the store and commented on the unusually chilly atmosphere up there compared to downstairs, but could find no trace of the uniformed man. Never again did the victim of this particular haunting venture upstairs and never again did he arrive first for work for fear of being alone in the building.

METAL DETAIL

The Metal Detail is a long, single-storey building that contains a heat treatment area and a paint spraying shop. A wide variety of anomalous phenomena have been witnessed here. Reports received (from a number of different employees) included shirt-pulling, taps on the shoulder, the sounds of metal rivets thrown to the floor and whispering and whistling, all seemingly caused by invisible entities. One storeman's experience was particularly odd. He found a ladder blocking his way; it was leaning out from the top rack of an 8-foot-high parts bay. He was carrying a large box at the time and had to step around the ladder with his back to the rack behind him in order to struggle by. Once he had passed around the ladder, he put the box down to move the ladder but as he straightened up, to his amazement, the ladder was suddenly upright at a 90 degree angle as if held in place ... A lone security guard, on patrol outside in the early hours of the morning, was near the Metal Detail building when he had the weird experience of some unseen force grabbing the back of his trousers, pulling him violently backwards. He quickly spun around to confront his antagonist, but there was no sign of anybody there.

Apparitions have occasionally been seen in the Metal Detail. During the 1980s, a man working in the paint shop was startled to observe a stranger walking towards the treatment tanks wearing old fashioned Marshall's overalls. The worker followed this unknown man only to find no trace of the intruder.

CIVIL BUILDING

The Marshall family bought the fields on which the airport is sited back in the 1930s from the Church and soon started erecting buildings and creating a runway. The white-painted Civil Building, which is Grade II listed, dates from those times; it was built in 1938 and it served as civil control for the airport for a long while. It is where the offices of the Chairman of the Marshall Group are situated, so, as befits its status, it is well appointed with solid wooden doors and an impressive staircase, which has echoed to the sounds of ghostly footsteps on more than one occasion. The door handle to the Chairman's office, which is at the top of the stairs, has been seen moving (by the secretary) on occasions when the room is unoccupied.

A contract cleaning supervisor saw an apparition one morning at 6.45 a.m. out of the corner of his eye. It began with a feeling that someone was behind him. He described it as a big man, dressed all in black, framed in the doorway of the Chairman's office. At the same time he said that his hair was standing on end as though affected by a static charge and he felt an intense cold. As the supervisor turned around for a better look, he discovered that he was completely alone. Like many people who have a brush with the supernatural he had previously been a sceptic when it came to ghosts but this contact changed his mind.

Cleaners have told many strange stories about their experiences in the Civil Building, including talking coming from empty rooms that have just been cleaned and the mysterious airman seen walking from the front doors only to vanish near the low wall by the main road. There are at least two ghosts that haunt the inside of the building. One is that of a woman, said by the cleaners to be 'all in white with long hair'. Another is a man wearing a hat, seen reflected in the glass of the front door. Icy cold winds, often associated with haunted places, have been felt in the upstairs landing and objects have been known to disappear from right under the cleaners' noses, never to be seen again ...

AIRPORT HOUSE

Machine Shop 1 is notorious for its 'Grey Man' but the Marshall Group site is also home to a 'Grey Lady' and she haunts Airport House, which was formerly a hotel before its many bedrooms were converted into offices and later on (in 1991) part of it was converted into a computer centre.

It was at the end of the lunch hour, one sunny day, when a young secretary was returning from her break. As she entered Airport House via the double set of front doors she saw a woman on the other side of the inner doors, about 4 feet away. The lady was tall with a pale face and fair hair and she wore a long dark dress. To the secretary's amazement this vision began to fade away right in front of her eyes. It was only then that she began to feel frightened and realised that she had met a ghost. Shortly after confiding her story to David Curry the young woman left the company.

A computer programmer was working on his own one night in order to complete an urgent project and by the time he had finally got ready to leave the building it was gone midnight. As he made his way down the dark corridor, lit only by some faint light from the landing windows, he suddenly felt an icy wind that seemed to have come straight from the Arctic. It was strong enough to blow him back against the passage wall, then as suddenly as it had come it was gone again, moving down the passageway. Thoroughly shaken by the phenomenon, the programmer ran blindly down the stairs and out of the front door in next to no time.

Several cleaners have also encountered the 'Grey Lady'. Sometimes she makes her presence known by a distinctive rustling sound. The most impressive demonstrations of her haunting abilities were reserved for a long-serving male cleaner, who had two unforgettable encounters with the entity. Early one morning he was busy unlocking all the rooms. As he moved down the corridor unlocking the rooms and opening them he heard and saw the doors being slammed shut one by one behind him. On another occasion he saw the apparition of the Grey Lady walking down the stairs. It is small wonder that he refused to go back in the building for some years afterwards!

The Marshall Group and Cambridge Airport have indeed provided a remarkable catalogue of ghostly experiences, something that contributes heavily to Cambridge's reputation as a most haunted town at the heart of a most haunted county ... welcome to *Paranormal Cambridgeshire*!

CHAPTER TWO

Cambridge 'Gown' – Unquiet Spirits in the Colleges

COLLEGE DEVELOPMENT

I cannot claim any strong personal links to Cambridge other than a deep affection for this vibrant, attractive capital of the county of Cambridgeshire. Its history stretches right back to Bronze and Iron Age times. The Romans were here in AD 43 and a settlement grew up near their fortified camp at Castle Hill. The Danes, who came in 875, were another influence on the growth of the town, which became a trading centre between East Anglia and the rest of the country. The Normans followed on; soon after their invasion they built a castle in an attempt to contain the Saxon outlaws of the Fens. In the Domesday Book the town was named Grantbridgechester. During the twelfth century, the town continued to grow in importance as a regional centre and new churches were constructed, including one of the modern town's landmarks, the Round Church, built in 1107, whose proper name is the Church of the Holy Sepulchre.

From 1209 onwards the scholars came to Cambridge, many having fled from Oxford after riots between the townspeople on the one hand and students and their teachers on the other. Between 1231 and 1271, the University of Cambridge became established, with its own Master and Chancellor, its own statutes and some measure of royal patronage. By 1284 the first College (later known as Peterhouse College) was established, so that students could both work and live in an environment conducive to learning. The Bishop of Ely bequeathed money to the scholars enabling them to buy land and add a dining hall. New colleges developed slowly. Between 1324 and 1354 another six colleges were founded. In 1441, there was further growth when Henry VI established King's College and the shell of King's Chapel started to be built, but his plans were disrupted by the Wars of the Roses with a consequent lack of funds and then he was deposed in 1461. It wasn't until 1508, when Henry VII was in power, that the completion of the shell of the buildings was completed. By the end of the fifteenth century a further five colleges were added. The whole character of Cambridge was changing from a market town to a centre for learning. The city was known as a place of two distinct communities – 'town and gown', the merchants/other townspeople and the academics.

The Reformation and the Dissolution of the Monasteries benefited the colleges, who were offered many of the houses that had previously belonged to the monks and friars. (This despite a report in 1545 that recommended the colleges should follow the same fate as the monasteries!) In 1544, during Henry VIII's reign, King's College Chapel's interior was finally completed. It is regarded as one of the greatest examples of late Gothic English architecture. During the next two hundred years no new colleges were founded but the academic reputation of Cambridge kept growing, making it the only serious rival to Oxford. Sir George Downing, whose grandfather had built 10 Downing Street in London, died in 1749, leaving a bequest to build another Cambridge college but a series of legal disputes delayed the release of the funds and Downing College was not begun until 1807. The latter part of the nineteenth century saw a further five foundations, including the first British women's colleges in the villages of Girton and Newnham.

The twentieth and twenty-first centuries have witnessed a rapid expansion of higher education. Cambridge boasts over thirty colleges with some sixty specialist subject libraries, more than thirty laboratories and ten museums as well as the university's own library and botanic gardens. The University of Cambridge can lay claim to sixty-eight Nobel Prize winners for science amongst its alumni – more than any other institution. Watson and Crick discovered the structure of the DNA molecule in 1953 in the Cavendish Laboratories in Cambridge, for which they were awarded the 1962 Nobel Prize award. The university has worked on the world's largest solar hydrogen project, aimed at powering environmentally-friendly hydrogen fuel-cell buses.

The town has developed significantly too, gaining an international reputation for 'high tech' industry and research in electronics, engineering and medicine. It is a prosperous place with a high standard of living and property prices that rival those of London. For those of us who have a particular interest in Cambridge College ghosts, I would recommend my favourite book on the subject, Robert Halliday and Alan Murdie's *The Cambridge Ghost Book*. For me it has proved to be an invaluable work of reference on the subject and it is a privilege to know Alan personally.

JESUS COLLEGE

The University of Cambridge (and its many colleges), with over 700 years of history, has more than its fair share of ghosts. Some of the colleges have interesting legends attached to them but I have concerned myself primarily with those sites that have factual reports of haunting attached to them. Some of the legends are of great interest however. Jesus College, for instance, has a ghost story associated with it that is pure fiction, yet many people over the years have come to accept it as fact! It concerns the 'Everlasting Club', formed in 1738, with an exclusive membership of just seven Fellows of Cambridge. These young Fellows, aged between twenty-two and thirty, would be Corporeal Everlastings during their lifetimes and in death they would remain members, as Incorporeal Everlastings. They met in a study on G staircase, which was nicknamed 'Cow Lane'. Could this be because prostitutes (or cows) were, at one time, smuggled into this part of the college? Credence was lent to this ghost story by the fact that the study on G staircase remained empty and locked for many years. It was finally opened up and became tenanted in 1924 and it remains tenanted to this day. The mystery of why it was left secured and untenanted for so long led to its being called 'The Ghost Room'. This probably fired Arthur Gray's (author of this tale) imagination to create his work of fiction to explain the mystery.

Drunkenness and debauchery were the hallmarks of the Everlastings. Their riotous meetings took place annually on All Souls' Day, 2 November. During the course of the next twenty-eight years, six of these young men died until, in 1766, only Charles Bellasis remained, as a Corporeal Everlasting. On the night of All Souls he locked himself into his study on 'Cow Lane' and at ten o'clock 'blasphemous outcries and ribald songs … aroused from sleep the occupants of the court'. At midnight all sound ceased in Bellasis' study and the light went out. Next morning the room

Jesus College, Cambridge, home to the fictional 'Everlastings'.

revealed a scene of utter chaos with seven chairs about the table, some of which were overturned. In the chair at the foot of the table was the dead Secretary of the Everlastings. The register of the club was on the table, signed by all seven members of the club … but how could that be possible? Bellasis's study was locked and never used again for the next 158 years. It is a great ghost story, but as mentioned earlier, entirely a work of fiction, dreamt up by Arthur Gray, Master of Jesus from 1912 to 1940. Perhaps the multitude of true ghost stories surrounding Cambridge provided the inspiration for the many works of fiction? As well as Gray, M. R. James, one of the greatest short ghost story writers of the twentieth century, was also a product of Cambridge. Montague Rhodes James was a fellow of King's College, and later became Vice-Chancellor of Cambridge. In his spare time he produced classic short stories, which continue to be used both on film and on television.

GIRTON

Girton College is named after the village where it is located, two miles to the north-west of the city centre up the Huntingdon Road (A604). The red brick and terracotta buildings are in the Gothic style, mainly hidden from the road by a dense screen of trees. There is more space here than in the city centre colleges, with well-kept grounds, including sports fields set in 50 acres at the southern end of the village. The plentiful trees provide a screen from the continuous roar of traffic passing by. The college was originally sited at Benslow in Hitchin, Hertfordshire, where it opened in 1869, before moving to the present site in 1873. The Cambridge site was on an Anglo-Saxon burial ground and during some excavations a student sighted the ghost of a 'Roman soldier' one evening in the grounds. The sighting gave rise to speculation that this may have been misidentification and the 'Roman' may in fact have been an Anglo-Saxon warrior.

Girton's most famous ghost, however, is the 'grey lady' and the Grey Lady Staircase is named after this apparition. A small block was added to Girton in 1876, known as the Taylor Knob because it was paid for by Mr Thomas Taylor. His daughter was one of the select few to be allowed to study at the university, but she became ill and died before she could take up her place. Shortly afterwards a group of students claimed to have seen an apparition of a grey lady on the spiral staircase in Taylor's Knob and it was believed to be the spirit of the unfortunate Miss Taylor. With the advent of the twentieth century and the introduction of electric lighting in the college there were no further reports of either 'Roman' soldiers or 'grey ladies'.

SIDNEY SUSSEX

Sidney Sussex College, founded in 1594, is famous as the seat of learning where Oliver Cromwell received his education and he later represented Cambridge as its Member of Parliament. The college is situated in Cambridge city centre, about midway between the Round Church and Market Hill. It has one of the most famous stories of all the many Cambridge hauntings, which was reported back in November 1967. In 1960, the embalmed head of the Lord Protector was presented to Sidney Sussex College by Dr Wilkinson and it was laid to rest in a secret spot in the ante-chapel, its presence being commemorated by a nearby plaque. In 1660, two years after Cromwell's death, the Restoration of the Monarchy was established. Cromwell's body was exhumed and hanged, and then his head was removed and mounted on a pole in Westminster Hall, London. It remained here for twenty years before it blew down in a great storm. The head then changed ownership a number of times before coming into Dr Wilkinson's possession.

Our story begins at 1 a.m. on 1 November 1967 – around the time of Halloween that most appropriate of haunting times. Third-year student John Emslie went to visit his friend Peter Knox-Shaw at Sidney Sussex. He decided to wait and to read in Knox-Shaw's room until his friend returned and as he waited he felt a presence and saw a partial apparition – what looked like a large mouth. At the same time Emslie sensed a gripping feeling in his neck and he also felt cold. Next he saw a floating, pale yellow, emaciated head without ears. The terrified student fled the room, close to panic. Some time afterwards Knox-Shaw himself returned, unaware of his friend's experience. He later recalled that on entering his room he experienced both cold and fear, without any logical reason. The strongest impression, however, was of a pungent, peculiar smell, but he saw nothing. He left his room again and soon bumped into Emslie. The two friends compared notes and Emslie recalled that he, too, had noticed the smell, which was like slightly rotten raw meat.

Linda Nield-Siddall was alone and half dozing at about 4.30 p.m. the next afternoon in her fiancé's, Mike Howarth's, room on the third floor, directly above that of Knox-Shaw. She looked up to see near the light switch, a large pale-blue and purple eye. This eye continued to come and go for some ten minutes. Linda was unaware of the events of the previous evening but was nonetheless nervous and left her room in a hurry. A number of similar incidents were experienced by other students including another sighting of the eye and reports of unusual coldness. This led Knox-Shaw, Emslie and Howarth and his friends to attempt a séance in Howarth's room one night. Unfortunately, about twenty members of the Cambridge University Psychical Research Society interrupted proceedings and the group of friends holding the séance broke up. Despite the aborted séance, no further sightings were recorded at Sidney Sussex. The witnesses to these strange events never varied their testimony. Over twenty years later the writer Geoff Yeates managed to track down two of them to interview for his book *Cambridge College Ghosts*, and they stuck by their strange story. Their view was that the paranormal events were directly connected with a student who had studied at the college in 1616, but never completed his degree, one Oliver Cromwell.

Sidney Sussex College, Cambridge, was haunted by Oliver Cromwell.

The apparition of an unknown lady was regularly seen and heard in Emmanuel House.

EMMANUEL

Emmanuel College lies just outside the busiest part of the city, on the east side of St Andrew's Street, not far from the central bus station. It stands on the site of a Dominican priory and was founded in 1584 by Sir Walter Mildmay, Chancellor of the Exchequer to Queen Elizabeth I. Many of Emmanuel's early members emigrated to America. John Harvard was among the ranks of those who moved to New England. Tragically, he died young and bequeathed half of his estate and his extensive library for the founding of the college in Boston, Massachusetts, that bears his name. Emmanuel has a reputation for producing some fine judges, scientists and writers. In 1667, the Brewhouse was completed in the eastern corner of the college grounds and in the 1880s the Hostel, to the south of the Brewhouse, was constructed. For almost a century the northern part of the Brewhouse, Emmanuel House, was rented to outside tenants. Many tenants were disturbed by ghostly activity before the building was eventually demolished in 1893. In 1867, a widow called Mrs Harris took over the lease on Emmanuel House with her children. It wasn't too long before she was hearing unexplained heavy, stamping footsteps in the passage outside the first-floor drawing room. The noises would continue down the stairs into the hall, where they abruptly ceased. Nothing was ever seen to account for these spectral sounds. Both Mrs Harris and members of her staff experienced this phenomenon on a number of occasions. A visiting friend, Mrs Dunn, was reading alone in the drawing room one summer's day when she, too, heard the phantom footsteps. As the door to the room was open, Mrs Dunn got up and looked out into the passageway. The 'peculiar loud steps', as she later described them, continued along the passageway and on down the stairs but without any visible signs of their originator. Mrs Dunn later became convinced that three suicides had been committed in Emmanuel House, which may be true, but there is no historical evidence to support this claim.

Eventually, a ghost was seen rather than heard at Emmanuel House. Mrs Harris had been living there for about three years when her daughter-in-law, young Emily, came to stay and she was deliberately kept uninformed about the weird footsteps. The girl was in bed one evening when she looked towards the dressing table and standing there, illuminated by the light reflected from a streetlamp, was a short figure wearing what appeared to be a bridal veil. Emily said that she felt 'creepy and crawly' as the figure stood there, unmoving. The girl ducked under the bedcovers for some time and when she emerged the apparition had vanished.

Another youngster was badly frightened by an Emmanuel House haunting. This time it was Mrs Harris's pageboy and great pains had been taken to keep the lad in ignorance of the house's reputation as he was new to his job. One night he awoke to something in his bedroom that scared him so that he screamed out loud.

Sadly the little lad later had a fit, became ill and left the house for good shortly afterwards. Mrs Harris moved out in 1875.

Short tenancies followed, possibly due to the unseen and unwelcome guests, until Miss C. M. Bowen, sister of Mrs Dunn, took up residency in the 1880s. Miss Bowen was said to be sceptical about ghosts. She had two ghost-free years then, one evening, as she sat writing in the dining room on the ground floor, she heard someone descending the stairs. When no-one appeared she went out into the entrance hall but could find no trace of anyone. Miss Bowen returned to her writing but shortly afterwards the same thing happened again. This time she called out and got up to see who was coming downstairs. Once again there was nobody to be seen and it later emerged that a servant, Kate Skipton, had also heard the footsteps. She was described as 'middle aged, sensible and decidedly unimaginative', yet this servant had another brush with the paranormal when she clearly heard an unfamiliar voice call out 'Kate' from the general direction of the attic stairs when she was in her bedroom. She looked out of her room but there was no-one about. This happened on more than one occasion.

In 1884, Miss Bellamy, a teacher who worked for Miss Bowen, was standing in the kitchen, looking towards the garden door, when she saw a stranger, a lady, descending the stairs. This woman crossed the hall and turned in the direction of the dining-room door. Two things stood out for Miss Bellamy, the smooth, gliding movement of the lady and the fact that, although she passed within a few yards of her observer, there were no sounds whatsoever. Miss Bellamy later admitted to 'an uncanny feeling being communicated to her'. She followed in the direction the stranger had taken and even went into the dining room, but there was no trace of the mystery woman. Miss Bellamy was considered a 'strong-minded individual', a typical board schoolmistress, who had no prior knowledge of the haunting of Emmanuel House. She was certainly not the type to indulge in flights of fancy and had no reason to invent such a story. Miss Bowen (and her school) left the property in 1885 after just four years tenancy. We have Eleanor Sidgwick, mathematician, later Principal of Newnham College and member of the Society for Psychical Research to thank for much of the details of the story, collected from letters received from Mrs Harris, Mrs Dunn and Miss Bellamy. Eleanor's husband was Henry Sidgwick, Professor of Moral Philosophy at Trinity College. He was elected president when the SPR was founded in 1882 and his principal colleagues in the SPR were Frederick William Henry Myers and Edmund Gurney, also Fellows of Trinity.

Little is known about the period between 1885 and 1893, when the haunted building was demolished, as Mrs Sidgwick was not in touch with the later tenants. The ghosts seem to have disappeared along with the rubble of the old building since there have been no phenomena reported at the new site.

CORPUS CHRISTIE

Corpus Christie is unique in that it was founded in 1352 by the townspeople of two guilds. All other Oxford and Cambridge colleges were either founded by the aristocracy or the clergy. A licence was procured from Edward III for the College of Corpus Christie (Body of Christ) and the Blessed Virgin Mary. This college is one of the oldest and smallest in Cambridge University with some 230 undergraduates. It lies on the east side of Trumpington Street, not far from Lion Yard shopping centre. The Old Court (a court is a quadrangle) was begun in 1352 but it took another twenty-five years before it was completed in 1377. New Court was later added, in 1823, but it was completed rather more quickly, by 1827. Notable scholars included playwright Christopher Marlow, Sir Nicholas Bacon (father of Francis Bacon) and Thomas Cavendish, who, during 1585 and 1588, became the second Englishman to sail around the world.

The beginnings of Corpus' famous ghost story are thought to originate in the seventeenth century. The Black Death had returned in 1630 when Dr Henry Butts, a Doctor of Divinity, was Master of Corpus Christie. Everyone fled the plague

Corpus Christie College, Cambridge, has been the scene of 'harrowing and gruesome' hauntings.

but Dr Butts remained at his post, alone. He lived in the Master's Lodge in the south-east corner of Old Court. It was here that he hanged himself, on Easter Day, 1 April 1623, with a noose made from a handkerchief. For many years afterwards the upper rooms near the kitchen in Old Court had the reputation of being haunted. It wasn't until 1883 that records of the hauntings were kept. This was when a freshman (first-year student), Walter Moule, took up residence in what had been the old Master's Lodge on the same staircase as his uncle, Charles Moule, who had become Senior Fellow in 1879. Charles Moule had been plagued by strange, unaccountable noises in his room when he, too, had been an undergraduate. He was reluctant to talk about it, so the story went, because he had been obliged to 'crawl out of his rooms on hands and knees' in sheer terror on one memorable occasion. His nephew recorded hearing loud bangs 'like a trapdoor falling' and one night his friend Eric Lewis, who was living in adjacent rooms, came to take refuge with Walter Moule after becoming terrified by mysterious loud noises. Moule, who later became a missionary in China, calmed his neighbour by praying with him.

Two college chefs, Body and Porcheron, also reported ghostly occurrences. At one time it was so bad that no servant would stay alone in the kitchen at night for fear of seeing an apparition. Footsteps and wall-rappings were heard on occasion, but in the Michaelmas term of 1903 the audible phenomena not only became louder but also more frequent. One unfortunate undergraduate was woken from his sleep by a cacophony of knocking accompanied by violent shaking of the washstand at the foot of his bed. The *Cambridge Daily News* picked up on the story, which appeared in the 24 February edition, 1904:

> Last term in the small hours of the morning an undergraduate in the old part of Corpus Christie College saw something of a supernatural appearance. It so unnerved him he became quite ill; he refused to continue to occupy the room and moved to another staircase. Naturally the college authorities deemed it desirable to prevent the story from gaining publicity and until now have succeeded in suppressing the circumstances. But now the harrowing and gruesome facts have leaked out and the recent visitation of 'something' to the undergraduate is beyond dispute.

Events took an interesting development in the following Easter term. It was about 3 p.m. when student Llewellyn Powys, who later became a prominent writer, returned to his rooms (which were situated opposite the reputedly haunted rooms in Old Court) to do some work. He found it hard to settle down to his studies due to a strong sense of unease and he felt strangely drawn to the window. As Powys looked out across the quadrangle he saw the head and shoulders of a man leaning out of the window opposite. The man was a complete stranger, who had long hair and who glared at the Welshman, while remaining motionless. Powys later recollected observing the unmoving stranger for several long minutes before rushing to his bedroom for a better viewpoint. The long-haired man was nowhere to be seen and Powys dashed to the rooms opposite, knocked repeatedly and called out but there was no response. It wasn't until that evening before he could quiz Milner, who occupied the rooms opposite, only to find that he had been out for the whole afternoon from two o'clock. His bed maker didn't arrive till 6.30 p.m. and nobody could have been in his rooms between 2 and 6.30 p.m.

During the next few months the haunting increased, both in intensity and frequency. At 5 a.m. one morning, an undergraduate in the rooms below Milner awoke to discover a white figure standing motionless beside his bed, where it remained for several minutes before vanishing through the closed sitting-room door. The frightened witness hurriedly dressed and left his rooms. On a later occasion this unfortunate young man was plagued by 'loud and intimidating noises' that forced him to seek out the company of a friend. Eventually, when he had calmed down sufficiently, the student returned to his rooms but upon opening the door he saw the ghostly figure of a man standing by the fireplace. He made another hurried exit and spent the remainder of the night trying to snatch some sleep on his friend's sofa. The very next day he demanded to be moved from his haunted rooms. He was re-accommodated and his rooms, unsurprisingly, remained empty for some time afterwards.

At another part of Old Court a young man who was studying for the priesthood, Arthur Wade, was tormented by noises every night over a period of several months. His friend John Capron, also studying for the priesthood, agreed to help him to conduct an exorcism. They were joined by John Randolph Leslie, known as Shane Leslie, who was from a wealthy landowning family in Ireland and a cousin to Winston Churchill. Shane Leslie was also a member of Cambridge Psychical Research Society. Wade, Capron and Leslie conducted their exorcism in October 1904. Capron armed himself with a phial of holy water and Wade had a crucifix. The ceremony was conducted in the dark room, lit only by the embers of a dying fire. The three ghost hunters knelt together and recited the Lord's Prayer. Capron raised his crucifix on high and called on the three persons of the Holy Trinity to command the spirit to appear. It was then seen by Capron and Wade but not immediately by Leslie, who later reported that he felt the hair rising on his neck and a prickling in his scalp. The other two saw 'a mist, about a yard wide, that slowly assumed the shape of a man, shrouded in white with what appeared to be a gash on his neck'. (Could what appeared to be a 'gash' in the dimly lit room have been a handkerchief perhaps?) The visitation then moved slowly around the room. The three students approached it with cross held high in protection, while Capron sprinkled holy water about the room, but as he did this they were all hurled back by some unseen force. All three then saw the apparition framed in the open doorway and described it as a 'strangely menacing appearance which appeared cut off at the knees'. The three friends gripped each other tightly for support and as they did so the apparition dematerialised.

Convinced that 'the thing' had moved upstairs Capron led the group up to the room of a medical student, Hugh Milner, who was a known atheist and a complete sceptic about the supernatural. The medical man was calmly reading when the trio burst into his rooms, Capron brandishing the crucifix. The medical student darted in front of him and before any warning could be given he collapsed on the floor, mumbling that he felt extremely cold. This was Shane Leslie's first encounter with a ghost and it is interesting to speculate if this incident affected his decision to convert to Roman Catholicism while at Cambridge. The young Leslie went on to become Sir Shane Leslie, a distinguished writer and diplomat. One of his works was *Shane Leslie's Ghost Book*. His answer to the question 'Do the dead know when they haunt the living?' is intriguing. He writes, 'It is possible that they are aware, but the tremendous authority of St Thomas Aquinas favours the view that the dead are not aware of their own apparitions. Other spirits may be acting the part. In this St Thomas has touched one of the stumbling blocks of modern Spiritualism. Manifestations may be genuine but not the manifestor.'

The college authorities tried to keep a lid on the hauntings and the exorcism, so the affected rooms were closed temporarily but eventually an American student named Taylor occupied one set of vacated rooms, rent free, and no harm seems to have come to him. The notoriety of the haunted rooms, however, meant that many visitors would gather on a Sunday afternoon at the railings surrounding Old Court to look up at the rooms of ill repute. Eventually, as time passed, the fuss died down and the strange affair was forgotten. No hauntings have been reported from Old Court since those far off times. One interesting footnote, however, is the strange appearance of the manifestation, seemingly cut off at the knees. The three undergraduate amateur exorcists were unaware of a letter written by a Fellow of Corpus Christie in 1642, just three days after Dr Butts' suicide. The letter describes the circumstances in which the body was found, 'he tied the handkerchief about the superliminare of the portal ... which was so low that a man could not go through it without stooping; and so wilfully with the weight of his body strangled himself, his knees almost touching the floor.'

PETERHOUSE – CAMBRIDGE'S MOST HAUNTED COLLEGE

My favourite ghost story from the Cambridgeshire colleges concerns Peterhouse, Cambridge's oldest (founded in 1280) and smallest college, with only 284 undergraduates. It is also the most recently haunted and has been subject to at least three exorcisms during its history. The college hit the headlines in December 1997 when consideration was given to calling in an exorcist as dons were concerned that 'the ghost sightings were impairing the smooth running of the institution'.

Peterhouse lies to the west of Trumpington Street and north of the Fitzwilliam Museum. The east-facing frontage is dominated by the college chapel that stands between the library and the Burroughs building behind ornate cast-iron railings. Across the street from the chapel is the Georgian Master's Lodge, bequeathed in 1726, and behind that is Cosin Court, the newest building on the site. When the college moved to its present site in 1284 it stood next to St Peter-without-Trumpington-Gate. The church was renamed St Mary the Less in 1340, but the college retained its name of St Peter's College. Peterhouse has an illustrious past; former students and Fellows include Thomas Gray the poet, Charles Babbage, inventor of the 'difference engine' (regarded as the earliest computer), Sir Frank Whittle, inventor of the jet engine, and Sir Christopher Cockerel, inventor of the hovercraft.

Paranormal investigators should visit a quiet corner of the old courtyard overlooking the graveyard at Peterhouse, which still has the power to spook some people. On the outside wall of the dormitory there is an adjacent stone gate and across from that is the cemetery. Sightings of a dark figure crouching on top of the stone gate have been reported since the 1700s. This malign 'presence' was thought to have influenced students to commit suicide. Rumour had it that as many as ten students who lived in the dorms with windows facing the graveyard committed suicide after seeing the dark figure. During the 1960s, the university Dean brought in some priests and a ceremony was conducted to expel the malign presence. Interestingly, no more sightings were reported and no more suicides took place.

It was as early as the eighteenth century when the first exorcism was carried out at Peterhouse. Details are sketchy from those far off times but it seems that a student was being plagued by a poltergeist in his room. The exorcism was effective, which is often not always the case, but in this instance the presence was successfully banished. The beginnings of the most famous Peterhouse ghost story may also be traced back to these times.

On 17 August 1787 Edmund Law, Bishop of Carlisle and Master of Peterhouse, died. He had been appointed in 1754 and in accordance with the custom that existed into the twentieth century, he held that position until his death regardless of his mental and physical health. The election that followed was to provide a web of intrigue. It should be explained that a Fellow is an academic post in a college, as distinct from the university, and Fellows may be male or female. It was Senior Fellow and Bursar Francis Dawes' duty to organise this election, to be held on 31 August. With no suitable candidate from the north of England, Daniel Longmire, a vicar and former Fellow born in the north, was proposed. George Borlase, a younger Fellow and tutor from the south, was the other candidate. Longmire had helped the Bishop's older brother, Lord Hardwicke, and therefore felt confident of Bishop Yorke's support. Borlase saw the threat of Longmire and decided to introduce a third candidate. He and his supporters chose Francis Barnes, a Fellow

Peterhouse College, Cambridge. Cambridge's most haunted college.

Peterhouse's Stone Gate. A 'malign presence', which crouched on the top of this gate, was exorcised here some forty years ago. This 'dark figure' had reputedly adversly influenced Peterhouse students for over 200 years.

and Vice-Provost of King's College. Barnes was told that he stood no chance of being elected Master of Peterhouse. His role was to deprive the Bishop of an opportunity to appoint Longmire and leave the way clear for Borlase. As expected Borlase romped home – he was the popular choice. The election was later backed up by a petition to Bishop Yorke, made by two Fellows who visited Yorke to advise him that Borlase was the college's preferred choice for the position of Master. The Bishop had other ideas and he discovered that, as visitor to the college, he had the right to select a new Master without consulting the Fellows.

On 28 September 1789 Francis Dawes, then in his sixties, hanged himself from the bell ropes in the fifteenth-century turret that connects the Hall and the Combination Room. He left no note and no explanation for his suicide was given. It seems likely, however, that the highly respected classicist blamed himself for the election fiasco involving Francis Barnes as a candidate for Master of Peterhouse. A crowd of hundreds, including the Vice Chancellor, turned out for the funeral, held at neighbouring Little St Mary's.

In spring 1997, reports leaked out to the press about sightings of a ghost at Peterhouse, thought to be that of Francis Dawes. By that December *The Times* and the BBC had got the story, which quickly spread across the internet. Radio Four, the Ceefax service and television news reported the incident to the nation. Some of the staff at the college were refusing to enter the Combination Room, a thirteenth-century, oak-panelled chamber linked to the Fellows' Dining Room, where the apparition was last seen. Two butlers, Matthew Speller, aged twenty-two, and Paul Davies, aged twenty-six, witnessed the ghost's slow movement across the room before its disappearance near the staircase where Dawes' body is believed to have been discovered over 200 years previously. The butlers described the apparition as human sized but said it was impossible to distinguish features or to determine its sex. It floated about a foot off the floor but in the dimly lit room it stood out brightly and the witnesses experienced a sudden chill. This was in April 1997 while they were serving dinner one day; they had gone to the Combination Room to get some plates. On another occasion they interrupted a dinner to inform the Dean about another sighting. This time Davies had walked towards the figure but it did not waver, taking the same path towards the window. Speller and Davies were also witnesses to audible phenomena when they heard 'rhythmical knocking which appeared to move around the panelling'. Paul Cook, senior butler, was another who had a brush with the paranormal when he noticed a solid wooden door shaking violently. He tried his hardest to hold it shut but he had no effect and when the vibrations ceased and he could open the door there was nobody on the other side.

When asked by *The Times* in December 1997 about the butlers' report, the Dean of Peterhouse said, 'I saw the absolute terror on the faces of those two (butlers) so I don't doubt that something happened. In a college full of unreliable people, they are completely reliable.' Dr Andrew Murison, Senior Bursar, added, 'There is no reason to disbelieve the butlers. They are very level-headed.' A later incident involved Andrew Murison himself, who heard repetitive knocking one night at 11.45 p.m. and despite having a large fire in the room he was 'enveloped by an eerie chill'. He turned around to see a small man wearing a wide collar, holding a large hat. The figure stood there for a few seconds before dematerialising. Dr Graham Ward, theologian and Dean of Peterhouse, looked into the possibility of an exorcism. He was told by the local exorcist appointed by the Diocese that the only way to banish the ghost was to hold a full Requiem Mass in the presence of all forty-five Fellows and the kitchen staff. This was most unlikely to be arranged, particularly as some Fellows, particularly a few scientists, described as 'a cynical lot', would not agree to attend the Mass as they didn't believe in ghosts. It is thought that some kind of ceremony was carried out though, as reports of haunting at Peterhouse seem to have ... petered out.

As a paranormal investigator, what makes Cambridge so special for me is that the world's most respected paranormal investigation society came into being in this town. The Society for Paranormal Research was founded by five eminent thinkers, three of whom studied at Cambridge. The first SPR president was Henry Sidgwick, philosopher and Fellow of Trinity College. Psychic researcher and original SPR founder Edmund Gurney studied at Cambridge, as did a third SPR founder, the distinguished poet Frederic William Henry Myers. The SPR continues to follow its purpose, 'to understand events and abilities commonly described as psychic or paranormal by promoting and supporting important research in this area', and to 'examine allegedly paranormal phenomena in a scientific and unbiased way'. The SPR is based in London's Kensington, but its archives remain in Cambridge. Long may it continue its most valuable contribution to the study of all things paranormal.

In April 2010, another Cambridge man, the eminent parapsychologist Anthony Donald Cornell, passed away, aged eighty-six. Tony Cornell was born in Histon and educated at the Perse School and Fitzwilliam College. For many years he was president of Cambridge University Society for Psychical Research. He joined the Society for Psychical Research (based in London) in 1952 and became vice president in 1992. Tony became an authority on the paranormal and was a regular guest on television documentaries and television debates centred on the supernatural. His particular interests were hauntings, poltergeists and psychic mediums. Tony Cornell's reputation was built on scrupulous attention to detailed, careful investigation, allied to a healthy scepticism. Together with Alan Gauld and Howard Wilkinson he invented SPIDER – the Spontaneous Psycho-physical Incident Data Electronic Recorder – which utilised computing and audio-visual equipment. He was the co-author (with Alan Gauld) of *Poltergeists*, published in 1979. His magnum opus, however, was *Investigating the Paranormal*, published in 2002 – the result of over fifty years of research, which should be required reading for every serious student of paranormal investigation. He stated that of the 800 or so cases that he investigated only around 160 were 'difficult to explain' and of these 160 a mere handful 'seemed likely' to be of a paranormal nature.

CHAPTER THREE

Cambridge Town Hauntings

HAUNTED STREETS

Cambridge is an easy town to fall in love with; fortunately, I can visit it frequently as I live in nearby Royston, Hertfordshire. There are, however, some Cambridge streets that I wouldn't feel entirely comfortable walking alone in at night. All Saints Passage is one and that well-known cut-through to the Backs from the centre of town, Trinity Lane, is another. The medieval heart of the town, between Trinity, Gonville and Caius colleges, takes on a different persona after darkness has fallen and crossing the Cam suddenly seems quite unattractive. Christ's Pieces can be 'atmospheric' on a misty winter's night. At such times it is not difficult to believe the multitude of ghost stories associated with the county's capital. As is the case with other extremely old and extremely haunted towns and cities such as Edinburgh, York or St Albans, Cambridge has its very own Ghost Walk. It was inaugurated in 1998 and runs twice daily, starting at King's College (or the King's College of Our Lady and Saint Nicholas to give it its full title) between Thursday and Saturday. The organiser is my friend Alan Murdie, ex-chairman of The Ghost Club, one of Britain's oldest and most respected paranormal investigation societies. Alan is also a valued member of my own small paranormal research group, APIS (Anglia Paranormal Investigation Society). His fellow organisers are Robert Halliday, an archaeologist who was born in and who works in Cambridge, and Duncan Anderson, a former curator of the British Museum. Some thirty ghosts are mentioned on the walk.

The haunting is not confined to the colleges however; the streets themselves have their own paranormal phenomena. A ghostly smell of burning opium has often been reported from Fisher Lane, a narrow, medieval passageway in the heart of the city. The aroma has been described as resembling a strong perfume being burned. During the nineteenth century, bargemen and sailors lived in run-down lodgings in the area and they smoked opium which came from the docks at King's Lynn. An old sailor is known to have fallen into a drug-induced stupor and burned to death in his lodgings in the area of Fisher Lane, which runs by the side of the Pickerel Inn in Magdalene Street. This inn, which is allegedly the oldest in town, has a grim

Pickerill Inn, Magdalene Street, Cambridge. Three former landlords have committed suicide, two by hanging and one by drowning – and their presences are still felt.

history. Two previous landlords committed suicide by hanging themselves from a hook in the cellar. A former landlady chose drowning as the preferred method of ending her life. She threw herself into the Cam and her ghost has been seen and her presence felt by a number of members of the pub's staff. Other hauntings from Magdalene Street include a report from 1967 when two people working in an office there saw the ghost of an elderly man in a nearby house. The witnesses were not from Cambridge and knew nothing about the history of the area. Locals were able to match their description with a former resident who had committed suicide in the property in the 1950s.

In March 2009, reports appeared in the *Cambridge City News* about the haunted cellar at interior furnishings specialist Wallace King. Anglian Water was carrying out repairs in King Street. The water company used cameras to track the path of the King Street sewer and discovered a manhole cover in Wallace King's cellar. Andy Williams, a spokesman for the furnishers, said, 'One of the manholes they have sealed is in our very dark basement and the men who went down came back up looking very uncomfortable. We are not surprised though as the Wallace King building itself is steeped in history.' Part of the shop stands on the site of the stables that were owned by Hobson, the terse businessman who hired out horses and gave his name to the phrase 'Hobson's choice', which became synonymous with no choice at all. The water men claimed that when they were at work in the basement it turned unusually hot and then cold for no obvious reason. The door to an old cupboard was repeatedly wedged shut in its wooden frame, but it was always found to be wide open when they next visited the cellar. The road is now resurfaced and the basement has been closed up again, but behind the cellar door who knows if the paranormal activity has ceased ...

I am not a vegetarian. In fact, if there is such a thing I'm an enthusiastic 'meatatarian', but I would recommend the Rainbow Vegetarian Restaurant in King's Parade. My philosophy is that one should, after all, try everything once, so long as it is both legal and decent. I was surprised to find that I enjoyed the food here, particularly the delightful pudding. I was also surprised to learn from the staff about its paranormal reputation. Apparently coughing sounds and footsteps have been heard when there has been nobody about to account for these ghostly noises. A restaurant manager reported receiving a push from some invisible presence which propelled her into a passageway. Whatever it was she felt it was definitely 'unfriendly'. An apparition has been seen, briefly, by a member of the kitchen staff, who also described a smell of perfume, which lingered after the vision dematerialised. The general opinion seems to be that the Rainbow is haunted by the ghost of a woman who died in rooms above what is now the restaurant some twenty years ago.

St Mark's Vicarage in Barton Road is haunted by the ghost of a young serving maid. The story featured on Anglia Television's *Signs and Wonders of the Afterlife* in November 1997. Three generations of vicars attested to strange experiences in the vicarage. The first was Canon Bill Lovelace, who was resident from 1967 to 1987 before he retired to live in Swaffam Bulbeck. The Canon and his family regularly heard loud crashes and the noise of objects being moved about in the attic. His wife Betty saw the figure of a young girl at the foot of her bed. The Canon said, 'The vicarage used to be much bigger and was divided in half about the time we moved in.' It was an interesting comment, since alterations to old buildings often seem to trigger ghostly activity. He continued, 'I believe the ghost is a young servant maid who is in some way not at rest.' He added, 'There was no feeling of evil and it was not in any way threatening.' Canon Philip Spence was the next occupant and he knew nothing about the Lovelace's experiences. The Spence family, who later moved to Peterborough, also experienced poltergeist activity. The most mysterious event was when a set of doilies were taken out of a drawer and placed under the glass of a 1930s bedroom furniture set. Monica Spence said,

'She was always doing helpful things and we did not feel frightened at all.' This may explain why none of the vicars decided to conduct an exorcism! The third vicar was Christine Farrington, who confirmed that the vicarage continued to be actively haunted with objects being moved, doors being opened and the central heating being turned on and off. When Christine first arrived here in 1996, she saw 'a forlorn young woman' standing at a window, but when the vicar went into the house it was empty.

Bene't (St Benedict's) Street is home to the Eagle pub, which dates back to the fourteenth century. This hostelry has a haunted reputation, with the apparitions of some young people seen here. Two boys, who died in unexplained circumstances, have allegedly been seen in an upstairs window. According to Robert Halliday and Alan Murdie, some of their Ghost Walk participants have told them about a girl who also appears from time to time in the Eagle. In 1959, she is said to have been seen surrounded by a glowing light, holding a lighted silver candlestick and in 1977 a 'Victorian girl dressed in black' was reportedly encountered on the staircase. It is not a Cambridge pub that I have frequented yet. One of the tables in the pub is said to tilt up without warning – a paranormal phenomenon that, as a lover of real ale, I might not appreciate!

Montague Road is famous for the story of Geoffrey Wilson's one and only ghost sighting. He was ten years old in the summer of 1924 when he saw a young woman swinging from a hammock in the summer house of his grandparents' home at number 25. He described the pretty, frail lady's appearance and wondered at his family's discomfort. The reason for their consternation did not emerge until some years later when he discovered that his description matched that of his paternal aunt Stella. But she had died of tuberculosis earlier that same summer of 1924.

Newmarket Road can lay claim to the most bizarre spectral sighting. People have claimed to have seen what looks like a ghostly penguin waddling up the road. Paranormal investigators have formed a theory that this apparition is not, in fact, a bird but a doctor with a cloak and a beak-like mask which would have been worn to avoid catching the plague known as the Black Death, which ravaged the town in the 1300s.

Michel's Brasserie, located in Northampton Street, was formerly the Oyster Tavern, where many strange things were reported, particularly around late 1979 and the early part of 1980. The phenomena included lights turning themselves on and noises heard in empty upstairs rooms. Downstairs an apparition was seen standing in the bar. It was described as having 'spiky hair and a high collar' and it was seen by two women who worked in the pub on two separate occasions.

Silver Street was the setting for an encounter with the 'otherworldly' in November 1954, when a student was returning to Queen's College one evening. Ahead of him he saw the stooped figure of an old man, holding his hands behind his back. The stranger had long silvery hair and was wearing a morning coat. When the student got within about 6 feet of the figure it just dematerialised. He wrote a report immediately on his return to his rooms, which he submitted to the Society for Psychical Research. The undergraduate was subsequently interviewed by the society's president, Professor Frederick Stratton, who remained convinced that this witness was telling the truth

Sherratt and Hughes was a haunted bookshop, thought to be one of the oldest in England before its closure in 1991. A Victorian man was sometimes seen browsing the aisles of books there. The best known haunted bookshop, however, is situated in St Edward's Passage. It sells second-hand books and it is actually called 'The Haunted Bookshop' (so named in 1986 after a sighting of a young girl at the head of the stairs by the owner). A 1997 television programme, *The Y Files*, featured the shop and a psychic investigator sensed a 'benign female presence'. A number of people, including several members of staff as well as a most recent owner, Sara Keys, have seen 'a charming young girl with long, flowing fair hair' and she appears to walk upstairs, but nothing is ever found on the upper floor to account for this presence. The apparition is accompanied by the smell of violets.

Cambridge has its own spectral hound, known as Shuck, which is said to frequent the Arbury Road part of the town; to see it is a portent of bad luck.

As a writer, libraries hold a special affection in my heart because I have spent many happy hours since childhood in a variety of these buildings. Cambridge Library in Lion Yard (built in 1975) was where I conducted some of my research for this present book. Readers of *Paranormal Hertfordshire* will know I have been involved in the investigation of two very haunted libraries in that county. It came as no surprise, therefore, to learn about the paranormal phenomena experienced at the old Cambridge Library when it was situated in Wheeler Street. The building was haunted by the ghost of John Pink (the first Borough Librarian up to 1905), which was reported as recently as 1992. The former library building (built in 1862) is now home to the Tourist Information Centre, but John Pink still seems to be keeping tabs on the place as objects have been inexplicably moved overnight while the place has been empty (of human habitation that is).

Corn Exchange Street is where the Red Cow (or the Communist Tart, as it is known to some local wags) is situated. This pub is host to one spirit not available in a bottle – a man is seen, but only from the knees upwards. It is thought that he walks on an earlier floor level, as the floors have been altered over the years that the building has been in existence. He was reported as recently as 1999 and some months after this a woman fled the bar when she sensed a malevolent presence. In October 2005, the Unicorn Steak and Ale House in Church Lane, Trumpington, was featured in the *Cambridge Evening News*. The landlord was interviewed and he claimed that ash trays were mysteriously moved about and on one occasion he found his clubs emptied out of his golf bag. As always, I am indebted to Robert Halliday and Alan Murdie's *The Cambridge Ghost Book* for some of the stories featured here. These authors' comprehensive knowledge of anomalous phenomena in Cambridge is unrivalled.

CAMBRIDGE'S FICTIONAL GHOSTS

Given the plethora of genuine haunting in Cambridge, it follows that this town has been home to many writers of fictional ghost stories. Arthur Gray, Master of Jesus College from 1912 to 1940, wrote *Tedious Brief Tales of Granta and Gramarye* (otherwise known as magic), which includes the unforgettable 'Everlasting Club' (which I've previously mentioned). E. G. Swain, Chaplain of King's College, published *Stoneground Ghost Tales* in 1912 and it was republished in 2009. Also republished in recent years is the work of former lecturer at Christ's A. P. Baker. His famous novella *A College Mystery* first appeared in 1918. The man most responsible, however, for bringing Cambridge and the supernatural together in the public consciousness was the former Provost of King's and Director of the Fitzwilliam Museum, M. R. James, who died in 1936. I treasure my copy of his wonderful short stories, classics of the ghost story genre. James wrote over thirty ghost stories in all; his best fiction has survived and has been televised. The protagonists are usually Cambridge academics, although the settings may be as diverse as a remote corner of Suffolk or some Continental village. James had a tradition of reading his stories aloud to a select audience of friends in his King's study every Christmas, no doubt warmed by a roaring fire and lit by flickering candles …

RADIO CAMBRIDGESHIRE

My good friends at Cambridge Paranormal Research Society were called upon in 2004 to investigate a haunted radio station in the town. I was particularly interested to learn all about this case as I had first-hand experience of investigating the studios at BBC Radio Three Counties in Luton, as detailed in my book *Ghostly Bedfordshire*. The station was opened in 1982, but one studio in particular had an odd atmosphere and a 'presence' was felt there. There were reports of unexplained flurries of chill winds in the corridors and disembodied voices calling out. On occasion, racks of tapes have been hurled by an unseen force across this studio. At night some disc jockeys refused point blank to broadcast from this studio or to even set foot in it. Martin Waldock, who runs CPRS together with Paul Brown, told me the whole story. At Halloween in 2004 the team, consisting of Martin, Paul, Angela Bloom Elaine O'Regan and Dave Fuller, conducted their second investigation at the studios in Hills Road and it was a fairly typical CPRS investigation.

As with all professionally conducted investigations, CPRS first carried out baseline tests to check the humidity, temperature, electro-magnetic fields and air pressure readings. Paranormal activity may affect these readings during the course of an investigation so it is essential to begin with an initial record of the environmental conditions. The EMF readings were not only varied but they moved around on the first floor, so the team set up a video camera here. Trigger objects were also set up. In the first-floor corridor Elaine drew around a coin and set it carefully down on a piece of white paper. It was to be checked later to see if it had moved. On the stairwell Angela set up a second trigger object, this time it was a ring. Angela believes that it is best to leave gender-specific objects, which the spirits may be able to relate to and women usually like jewellery. A third trigger object, another coin, was left in the second floor corridor. Elaine and Angela then used their dowsing crystals to try to pick up information about the spirits. Angela sensed a female adult and possibly an adolescent.

In the haunted studio (1a) yet more trigger objects, coins again, were set up, one was on a table in plain view of the webcam and another was placed near the presenter's desk. Staff have reported the presence of a male figure sitting in the presenter's chair. Sue Marchant, the nightshift presenter on BBC Cambridgeshire, was with the team. She is sensitive to the spirit world and is convinced that a friendly spirit looks after her as she presents the show. She looked around the studio with Martin and Dave but had to leave suddenly as her throat went very tight, which was both unpleasant and unusual. Dave was also affected; he felt a similar sensation as well as a pressure on the back of his neck.

There then followed some EVP (electronic voice phenomena) tests. By making recordings investigators sometimes pick up what are thought to be spirits trying to make contact. The team, together with some BBC staff, sat on the darkened first floor landing with the video camera pointing at them. Dave spoke to the spirits while Paul recorded. Dave used the standard paranormal investigator techniques, asking if anyone wanted to make contact and making assurances that the team were there out of interest and did not mean any harm. He then asked any spirits present to come forward, make a sound, speak or touch someone. The experiment was carried out again at 1.15 a.m. with the group sitting in a circle and holding hands as it is thought that spirits may utilise the group energy more easily like this in an effort to manifest in some way. The EVP recordings are later run through an audio analyser to see what results.

At 2.30 a.m. Elaine and Angela were sitting in the reception area when Elaine saw the shadow of a tall man, dressed in dark clothing, walk into the library. Angela saw the same thing, but walking out of the library. The sightings were made through the glass doorway so were not sharply defined. On checking to see where Paul and Martin were they found them in their chairs, where they had sat for some time and they had not been walking down the corridors.

At 3 a.m. Angela, Elaine, Martin and Paul returned to the first floor landing to try to make contact as they were certain that the spirit energy was in this part of the building but all remained peaceful for the remainder of the watch, as is so often the way at vigils!

The experiences of the BBC Radio Cambridgeshire staff, which occasioned the CPRS investigations, certainly make for interesting reading:

Jacqueline Sheriff, Broadcast Assistant

One Friday, after I'd done scripts and autocue, I came down the stairs from the studio to reception and half way down I thought I heard a gravelly voice say 'Hello'. I looked around to see who it was and couldn't see anyone around. I've noticed that these things always seem to happen on a Friday …

Ray Clarke, Afternoon Show Presenter

I was presenting the overnight show and was the only person in the building. It was 4.10 a.m., a record had just finished playing, I was talking and 'being a disc jockey' when I suddenly looked up and saw an apparition in the corner of the studio. There were no details or features to see, but it was the shape and size of an old lady. So … I was talking about this as the breakfast team was coming into work … and what I'd seen was an exact description of what had been seen before … and I'd never heard about previous 'visits'.

Catherine Rice, Director

I once recorded a radio play – a humorous look at God for the Huntingdon Writer's group – in the editing suite. I had loaded countless sound effects and music into our recording system to play out at the appropriate moments. There was one point where a sound effect was supposed to kick in, but the autoplay played 'Miserere Mea' by Allegri every time I pulled the switch. It wouldn't play anything else, even if I selected it. The weird thing is, after this point in the recording, everything else on the tape was wiped off when I played it back later. I had to get all the actors to come back in so we could do the second half of the play again …

Nick Young, Film Editor

The ghost spoke to me the other day, in the car park behind the studios … I was walking along the corridor towards the back car park, fumbling for my door fob, searching in my pockets, when a voice behind says something like 'Hang on, wait for me'. Then I felt someone behind me, and I could tell they were laden down with books or tapes or something. I was facing the door – I hadn't turned around – I was still going on about how I couldn't find the key and still fumbling about. When I turned around to see who I was talking to, there was no-one there.

Sue Marchant, Night-time Presenter

> I was a little late one morning for the Dawnbreaker show. I was getting a little
> hyperactive as I went into Studio 1A to change the trail sheets and had to do a double-
> take. There sitting in the chair was a figure of a man. A friendly gent sitting very
> calmly, dressed in beige with grey hair he was so calm he just gave me the message
> 'hey calm down'. Maybe he was the one who helped the morning I managed to lock
> myself out – luckily for the first time ever the early morning newsreader was here
> before 5 a.m. – I say cheers …

GHOSTS AT THE GUILDHALL

The Guildhall is a large and imposing, Grade II listed building situated at Peas
Hill, in the historic heart of the city, close to the thriving marketplace. It is run
and operated by Cambridge City Council and its Large Hall is used for a variety
of events, from live music and comedy through to craft fairs, conferences and
weddings. It has been in continuous municipal use for almost 800 years and the
Large Hall, on the south side of the building, dates back to 1872. In 1939, the
place was largely rebuilt, a suite of court rooms and cells were incorporated and
the Cambridge Crown Court was housed here until 2004. Cambridge Lending
Library was also accommodated within the Guildhall prior to its relocation to
Lion Yard in the mid-1970s. The Tourist Information Centre moved in to the area
formerly occupied by the library. In April 2009, another redevelopment of the
Guildhall began and Tourist Information moved to where the old Crown Court
had been. Jamie's Italian, a new Italian-themed restaurant created by Jamie Oliver,
now occupies part of the Guildhall.

A local paranormal investigation group, led by Adrian Atkins, has been
investigating this historic site for a number of years and they have discovered
that most rooms in the building have anomalous activity, which continues up
to the present day. The Large Hall is particularly active; the investigators have
catalogued a whole host of unexplained incidents. One night in April 2007,
several members of the team sensed the ghost of a girl. She was described as
having pigtails and was aged about nine years old. One person had their shirt
tugged and another had their hand held. An unseen orchestra was also heard
playing. Ade was busy setting up web cams on the stage when he heard footsteps
coming from behind the stage. The footsteps continued on into the hall, then he
heard them on the stage and the sounds passed him by but he could see no-one
and continued with his preparations. On another occasion the rancid smell of
vomit was detected by all of the team but within a few minutes it completely
disappeared. Noises were also heard coming from behind the curtains. The
following month, May 2007, another investigation was held and the Large Hall

was, once again, productive in terms of anomalous phenomena. A band was heard playing the Glen Miller classic 'In the Mood', and airmen were sensed, Americans on one side and British airmen on the other. Some five months later, in November (and again in December), the team returned for further intensive investigations. Unexplained door slamming was heard in the building. In a glass divination session heavy breezes were felt and the glass was seen to move, quite forcefully, across the table. The glass moved in the direction of the spot which the spirits claimed to be standing in.

Another active area of the Guildhall is around the cells. Dragging noises are often heard here and when a planchette was used the spirit of a suicide was picked up. A loud choking sound was heard too. Footsteps have also been reported, visitors have felt 'a charged atmosphere' and have also complained of headaches (which are sometimes associated with haunted sites). In the former courtroom mysterious knocks and bangs have been heard by both staff and investigators alike. On one vigil, when two investigators were on watch together in the courtroom, both of them heard an extremely loud bang right next to them. They said it sounded as though something had been thrown or someone had banged very hard on one of the nearby benches. Sharp temperature fluctuations were recorded on this and other occasions.

ABBEY HOUSE

One of Cambridge's most interesting buildings, both from an historical and a paranormal viewpoint, is Abbey House in Barnwell. It is a sixteenth-century mansion, built around 1580, located to the south of the river at the eastern exit of the town. It is situated close to the remains of Barnwell Priory, which was established in 1122. The name Barnwell means 'Children's Well' and it was home to both a Norman Priory and the Leper Hospital of St Mary Magdalene. The Priory was second in importance in East Anglia only to Ely Cathedral and it was once home to Augustinian Canons. It was sold off and destroyed during the Dissolution of the Monasteries in 1539. In Victorian times, the Barnwell area had completely different connotations, being associated with criminal activities and housing the majority of Cambridge's brothels! The present brick, stone and timber building is hidden by trees and a high brick wall.

Abbey House once had the reputation of being England's most haunted house, long before Borley Rectory claimed that particular distinction in the public consciousness. The reasons for this accolade may have been due to the number and variety of anomalous phenomena experienced here. At least six active ghosts were reputed to stalk this most spooky of locations. Then there are the many witnesses of sober and reliable character to these events. Both these factors lend weight to the supposition that this, in all probability, was (and maybe still is) the

Abbey House. Once infamous for being Britain's most haunted house and still haunted to this day.

most haunted house in Cambridge town. It is the only property that I know of which boasts a ghostly red squirrel amongst its spectral gathering. The squirrel has been reported running along the garden wall and then down onto the grass, but when approached it simply disappears. This is not the only spectral animal associated with the mansion. It is also home to a phantom hare, usually seen in wintertime, particularly when there is snow on the ground. It, too, is said to vanish when approached too closely.

The grounds are home to the shade of a nun, variously described as 'the black nun' or the 'grey lady'; she has often been seen walking along the pathway at the back of the house or lurking near the tall iron gates in the garden. A dubious and unsubstantiated story tells of an all too familiar legend – the nun who fell in love with a young man at the priory and was put to death for her sins. (The same tale is attached to Chicksands Priory in Bedfordshire – as recorded in my earlier work *Paranormal Bedfordshire*). An exorcism was conducted by priests in the mansion at the turn of the century, but as is often the case it seems to have been unsuccessful, since reports of the 'grey lady' are being recorded up till the present day. The so-called 'grey lady' has also been spotted in the vicinity of the grey stone wall, close by the tall iron gates, as well as the pathway at the rear of the property. The solid-looking figure of the lady in grey wasn't confined to the gardens, however, as we shall later discover.

During the years 1903–11, John Lawson, a Fellow of Pembroke College (who later became a First World War naval officer), lived at Abbey House with his wife Dorothy and their four children. Fortunately for modern-day investigators, Professor Lawson and his wife kept faithful records of their many supernatural experiences. These were gathered together (along with many succeeding tenants' written testimonies) by Frederick Stratton, who was Professor of Astrophysics at Cambridge University and President of the Society for Psychical Research between 1953 and 1955. Professor Stratton had first-hand experience of the haunting as he had rented Abbey House and lived there for some time. The Lawsons' haunting began as soon as they moved in on an October day in 1903, when they were greeted with loud banging on the bedroom doors that terrified the children and their nursemaids. At a later date heavy footsteps were heard on the staircase when there was nobody about to account for them. This became a most frequent occurrence. One of the guest bedrooms was completely shunned by visitors due to intolerable noises and an invisible presence that walked around the place. Faint voices and clanking chains were also reported from this same room. First the children and then later on the adults began seeing a small, brown furry creature, that the children christened 'Wolfie', running about the nursery. Interestingly the ghostly creature was always seen 'running about on its hind legs'. This may in fact have been the apparition of Jacob Butler's dog, which the eccentric lawyer is known to have trained to walk on its hind legs.

On one memorable occasion Dorothy felt herself being pulled out of her bed by an unseen force. She also claimed to have seen an apparition wearing full armour in her house. The nun/grey lady was seen in the garden by servants and visitors alike as well as the Lawsons themselves. This apparition's dark robes suggested to the family that she may have been a nun and it was noted that she appeared most frequently in the winter months. Peter Underwood's *Haunted Gardens* (Amberley Publishing, 2009) confirms the appearance of this apparition. A lady visited the grounds of Abbey House in recent times and she told Peter about her meeting with 'a lady in grey' who seemed to be quite substantial, until she suddenly disappeared. Enquiries revealed that no woman answering this description had either been a resident or a visitor to the house on that day.

Dr Frank Coles Phillips, who lectured at Corpus Christie, was the next occupant after the Lawsons. He observed the phantom furry animal, running along an upstairs floor on several occasions and some of his overnight guests complained of hearing footsteps and feeling something moving across the bed.

Inside Abbey House some truly unnerving visitations have awaited unwary guests. Sleepers have been awakened by quite terrifying phenomena. The most bizarre encounter was recorded in *Haunted Gardens*. During the 1920s, when the Ascham family were in residence, Mrs Ascham was shocked at the appearance of the disembodied 'deathly white' head of a woman that she saw floating in mid-air in her bedroom on no less than three occasions. Some people, while in bed, have felt 'something', variously described as either a heavy animal paw or a weighty tray being pressed down onto their chests, while others have had their bedclothes snatched away by invisible entities. Prior to the Aschams, at least two other tenants were said to have left the house in haste; one of these people left in the small hours of the night and who could blame them!

From the 1930s to the 1950s, a large number of tenants and their guests reported paranormal activity, including sightings of the nun and the unknown animal, at Abbey House. Activity seemed to be at its peak soon after a new tenant would arrive at the house.

Things were much quieter between 1965 and 1980 and it was assumed that the haunting had 'run its course'. It may be that the house's new owner, Professor Danckwerts, was in denial of any unexplained occurrences. This all changed in June 1980, however, when an elderly woman, who was a tenant of the professor, was woken in the small hours of the night. She reported seeing the apparition of a man, framed in a white light, who dematerialised as suddenly as he had appeared. This was followed by multiple apparitions, about six 'whitish, nun-like figures in procession'. Nothing quite like this particular haunting had been reported here before.

Weird things have been heard as well as felt: the movement of furniture, rapping, heavy footsteps, rustling and groaning noises. One spirit visitor to the bedrooms was known as the 'white lady' but this was a friendly ghost. It was reported to have tucked children up in their beds at night but, following an exorcism, she seems to have moved on.

One particular male presence has an identity. He has been recognised as the ghost of Jacob Butler, the so-called 'Giant Squire' (he was 6 foot 4 inches tall). Butler inherited the house in 1714 and he enlarged it quite considerably. He was a barrister and a noted eccentric who died in 1765 at the grand old age of eighty-four, soon after losing his beloved dog. The lawyer had himself buried in a giant-sized oak coffin, inside of which was a smaller, leaded coffin that contained his body. Jacob Butler was known as a generous and rumbustious character in life but he cuts a rather sadder figure in death, forever seeking, so it is said, the dog that he had loved so much. There have been numerous sightings of the unmistakable 'Giant Squire' with detailed descriptions of a tall man with a walking stick, wearing a black tricorn hat, long green coat with gold buttons, green breeches and black shoes with metal buckles.

The Abbey House became the Cambridge Buddhist Centre, when the religious sect bought the property in 2002. The Buddhists have since carried out extensive renovations to a building that had suffered years of neglect. Thus far the new owners have steadfastly refused permission for any paranormal investigations to be conducted in their home. Like all good haunted houses Abbey House continues to guard its secrets …

CHAPTER FOUR

Huntingdon Haunts

Cambridgeshire consists of four regions and we have investigated paranormal events in Cambridge. The other regions are Fenland, Peterborough and Huntingdon, which has its fair share of true ghost stories.

ALCONBURY

Situated around five miles north-west of Huntingdon, RAF Alconbury is a rare survivor from the RAF and USAAF's (United States Army Air Force) formidable presence throughout Cambridgeshire. Most of the original RAF/USAAF's thirty stations have reverted back to farmland, others have been covered over by industrial estates, some are now museums and others just gently deteriorate with the passage of time. All have a tale to tell and Alconbury is no exception. Having started operations in 1938 as a satellite of RAF Wyton, it became home to American bombers from the 8th Air Force. It is currently a non-flying facility under the control of the USAFE (United States Air Force in Europe) and with the exception of the period 1945–1951 it has been continuously in use. The USAFE also controls two other former Second World War bases. These are RAF Molesworth and RAF Upwood, which form the Tri-base area constituting the 423rd Air Base Squadron. Tri-base is so-called because of their close geographical proximity and interdependency.

Paranormal phenomena at Alconbury were witnessed by American security personnel during the 1970s. These included the sounds of unseen happy children, whose clearly heard voices sounded as though they were engaged in playing. One of the least expected things to hear at a military base perhaps. Research led to the discovery that in 1876, at nearby Abbots Ripton, at least fourteen people were killed in a train crash. Of these fourteen victims, six of the fatalities were children.

Searchlights at the base would inexplicably go out and a switch in a secure building was found to be mysteriously turned off. At the Rod and Gun Club on the base, figures in Second World War flying gear have been seen; it is said that the Rod and Gun Club building was the base mortuary during wartime. The Monks Wood area, also near to Alconbury, was notorious for sightings of monk-like figures.

In 1999, Alconbury's neighbour, RAF Upwood, was sold to Strawsons Property Services and in 2005 the last USAF family moved out of the Upwood housing area which was then redeveloped. The old briefing room at RAF Upwood was alleged to be another haunted location.

THE GEORGE HOTEL

Huntingdon was incorporated into the county of Cambridgeshire following boundary changes and the area in and around this town is now known as North West Cambridgeshire. One of the most attractive villages in this region is Buckden, just off the modern A1, or the Great North Road as it used to be known. Before that there was an even more ancient Roman thoroughfare, called Ermine Street, which was the main road to the north. During the heyday of the coaching era, in the seventeenth and eighteenth centuries, the Great North Road was a most important route as it linked London and York.

The George Hotel was built in the seventeenth century and was soon established as a stopping-off place for the coaching trade. It continued to benefit from coach travellers until the mid-nineteenth century when this mode of transportation was replaced by the railways. Then motor cars and motor coaches arrived, which continued to supply a constant stream of passing trade. The hotel was purchased in July 2003 by the Anne Furbank Group, and it closed a month later and remained closed for eight months during which time it was comprehensively refurbished. It was transformed into a modern brasserie, wine bar and hotel with twelve bedrooms. All of these beautifully designed bedrooms are individually characterised after their namesake of a famous 'George'. They include Bernard-Shaw, Eliot, Orwell, Best, Stubbs, Washington, Handel, Stephenson, Gershwin, Hanover, Mallory and Harrison.

This stylish new accommodation would be unrecognisable to seventeenth-century travellers and must have come as a shock to the ghosts of the old George Hotel. Back in the days when the hotel's bedrooms were numbered rather than named certain rooms were avoided by those of a nervous disposition. In the oldest part of the building rooms 100, 104, 105 and 112 were the focus of paranormal phenomena. These other-worldly encounters were witnessed by both hotel guests and staff. There were reports of an unseen nocturnal visitor who would lift up the bedcovers and pinch the legs of startled sleepers. Unexplained, heavy footsteps were heard and some doors were found to unlock themselves. In one case, from the late 1990s, a mother was awoken by her child, who started speaking in a gruff male voice. The lady cut short her stay and left the next day. On the first floor a man wearing a tricorn hat and a black coat was occasionally seen gliding along the corridor and on the main staircase the apparition of a woman was said to manifest.

THE GOLDEN LION HOTEL

The Golden Lion Hotel on Market Hill, close by the river in St Ives, dates back to the eighteenth century and it was a former coaching inn (like the George Hotel and also in common with the George Hotel it was also extensively refurbished in 2003). Two rooms are allegedly haunted here – rooms 12 and 15. In 1970, Cambridge Paranormal Society investigated poltergeist activity said to have been witnessed at the hotel. Andrew Green wrote about this in his book *Ghosts of Today,* which was published in 1980. A guest at the hotel reported seeing a ghostly lady in green while staying in room 12, which had long held the reputation of being haunted. Another apparition, this time of a soldier, allegedly from the English Civil War era, was seen gliding through a wall into room 15 by a chambermaid. Shortly afterwards the occupant ran out into the corridor insisting that he'd seen a figure in Royalist uniform which had then disappeared. This is interesting as the hotel dates from the eighteenth century and the Civil War took place in the seventeenth century, but then the building on this site may have had some other use? This is a case that may bear further investigation.

HEMINGFORD GREY

When I worked in Cambridgeshire I would often use the busy A14, travelling westwards, coming from the direction of Cambridge and then joining the A1 southbound to get to my home in Baldock. I used to pass the sign for Hemingford Grey and wondered about the origin of this unusual name. My research revealed that the strange name evolved over 200 years. Hemingford originated in Saxon times, 'the ford of the people of Hemma or Hemmi (presumably a Saxon chief)'. The Grey part came much later, from the de Grey family, who became the new lords of the manor in 1276. Situated on the south bank of the River Great Ouse, the village of Hemingford Grey grew considerably in the nineteenth century. After the Second World War, the population increased significantly.

The Norman Manor House of Payne de Hemingford was built in 1150 and it is thought to be the oldest continuously inhabited house in England. (It is in contention for this title with Chicksands Priory, Payne de Beauchamp's former home in Bedfordshire – see my earlier book, *Paranormal Bedfordshire*). One of its more recent well-known owners was Lucy Boston, author of the *Green Knowe* series of children's books, who died in 1990, aged ninety-seven. Her family, fortunately, preserved this special place. Lucy Boston fell in love with the old house when she first set eyes on it back in 1915. Polly Howat's book, *Ghosts and Legends of Cambridgeshire*, accurately details the history of the house and the associated hauntings. After the breakdown of her marriage in 1935, the author was in lodgings in Cambridge when a friend told her that the manor house in Hemingford Grey was up for sale. In 1938, Lucy Boston and her son Peter finally moved in to the dream home. The writer was aware of the manor's haunted reputation, which her household would soon experience at first hand. One room was designated as her music room, where stairs led to the attic. Servants would not use these back stairs or enter the music room when the place was empty. Some visitors, too, sensed a brooding malevolence in the house and were uncomfortable staying there for any length of time.

One fine spring day in 1939 Peter Boston was removing an extra floor from the music room when he felt an 'intense premonition of evil', which was so strong that he fled the room and made for the garden. The oppressive malevolent atmosphere remained in the room until the wall partitions were removed and the room was returned to its original design. The following summer, with the house now restored to its old shape, Peter was reading in the sitting room when he became aware of being surrounded by a number of people 'dressed in clothes of former periods'. This experience happened over a matter of seconds and it was 'as intensely pleasant as the previous year's experience had been wholly evil'. Were the former inhabitants of the house welcoming the return of their old manor?

Lucy Boston never saw her ghosts, unlike other visitors to the house, but she certainly heard them. At one time a phantom stick clattered over the banisters and rattled against the outside wall. A spectral flautist played in her music room from time to time and is reputed to play there still. During the Second World War, Lucy Boston did her bit for morale by entertaining the airmen from nearby RAF Wyton. She provided record concerts for these young men, with classical music played on her gramophone. At one of these soirees the company were feeling dispirited due to the fact that one of their aircrew had been killed the previous night. Loud footsteps were unexpectedly heard, descending the staircase, and then the door opened. Many in the assembled company swore that they saw the dead flyer walk in.

After Lucy Boston's death her son Peter and his wife Diana continued to live at the manor in Hemingford Grey. The hauntings continued, with ghostly singing and flute playing sometimes heard and a woman in a long gown was occasionally seen in the garden. The house is still open to the public, by prior arrangement, and it is well worth a visit, but if you are psychically sensitive be aware that you may tune into a powerful, invisible energy when you go there …

HINCHINGBROOK HOUSE

Persistent rumours about the haunting of Nun's Bridge have abounded for many years. The bridge, over the Alconbury Brook, is associated with nearby Hinchingbrook House because the nun that is supposed to haunt it is believed to originate at Hinchingbrook, which was a convent back in the twelfth century. Perhaps the best known encounter with the phantom was recorded in 1965, when a married couple who were crossing the brook reported seeing two ghosts on the bridge. One was dressed as a nun the other appeared to be attired as a nurse. The couple were adamant that they saw the phantom pair not once but twice as they also appeared on the bridge on the return journey. A myth has sprung up, as myths will do, that the nun took a monk as a lover and the two of them were subsequently executed for their crime. This story surrounds numerous other sightings of phantom nuns (read my investigation at Chicksands Priory in *Paranormal Bedfordshire*). There is no basis in fact for such a tale because there is no historical evidence whatsoever of monks and nuns being punished in such a way.

Hinchingbrook House itself is haunted too. It is the former home of the Cromwells before the Montagu family, Earls of Sandwich, purchased it and they in their turn sold the property to the County Council in 1962. The grounds were used for a hospital and a police control centre, while the house was restored and became Hinchingbrook School in 1970. Both sixth-form students and teachers have heard the ghostly voices of young children in the school. Further renovations to the house took place in 2009 and it is a matter of record that the builders refused point blank to work during the night time after several sightings of an apparition, thought to be a monk. The house is open for public tours on Sunday afternoons in the summer season, which gives everyone the opportunity to test out their psychic abilities and to see if they can detect any spectral presences.

HAUNTED PUBS OF SAINT NEOTS

The Royal Oak no longer stands at 38 High Street; like so many hundreds of other hostelries up and down the country, it closed its doors and the building had a change of use. Back in the 1960s, when it was still a pub, it became newsworthy due to a haunting that took the unusual form of a paranormal smell. It was rumoured that the building had already been subjected to an exorcism in the past, but in 1963 Mr and Mrs Hart, who had taken over the tenancy, were troubled by a psychic stink. When Mr Hart entered the old part of the building he started to whiff quite overpoweringly, yet when he moved away from this area the unexplained odour left him completely. The Harts were concerned that this unaccountable, unwanted aroma would adversely affect business and so a team of paranormal investigators conducted a séance in the public bar. The aim was to contact the spirit responsible for the nasty niff. The result of the séance was that the source of the awful reek was a man who had committed suicide in the old part of the inn. He had hanged himself from a meat hook and his body had remained undiscovered for a number of days and so the haunting took the form of the stench of rotting flesh, which had attached itself to Mr Hart. Another exorcism was held, this time successfully, as Mr Hart was never again troubled by odoriferous attachments.

The New Inn achieved fame as the location of the last stand for Royalist forces led by Henry Rich, First Earl of Holland, during the English Civil War. In 1648, Holland and 400 men retreated from Kingston-upon-Thames to St Neots. The next morning the Parliamentarians, under Colonel Scoop, arrived. Holland barricaded himself in the New Inn but the Roundheads gained access and arrested the Earl. The following day Holland was removed to Warwick Castle while the remainder of his Royalist force was removed to Hitchin. It has been claimed that several of the unfortunate Royalist officers were put to death near the New Inn. Given Colonel Scoop's reputation I would not be at all surprised. Holland was eventually taken to the capital and put on trial on 2 February 1649. The Earl was declared a traitor, sentenced to death and executed at the Tower of London. He maintained to the very end that the surrender of St Neots had been on condition that his life would be spared. If this was true then Colonel Scoop had behaved most dishonourably.

The New Inn continues to be haunted by the restless spirit of Henry Rich, Earl Holland. One night in 1963, long after closing time, the landlady of the New Inn, Mrs Kerr, went down on her own to the deserted bar. She was confronted by the apparition of a tall, slender man wearing an ankle-length cloak, which glided across the room and out through a closed door that led to the yard. Mrs Kerr checked the door but it was securely bolted from the inside, just as she had left it before going up to bed. She saw this same tall, cloaked figure on a number of occasions. Some customers have reported a feeling of great unease in the bar where Mrs Kerr's sightings were made. Does the Earl of Holland still return to the place where he was betrayed?

CHAPTER FIVE

Fenland Phantoms

FEN GEOGRAPHY

Fenland is a most atmospheric and tranquil region, almost a million acres of first-class agricultural soil (growing grains and vegetables) with wildlife-rich water that stretches from Cambridge to Lincoln and from King's Lynn to Peterborough. The rivers Welland, Witham, Glen, Nene, Cam, Great Ouse and Little Ouse made the Fens a vast inland waterway navigable only by shallow-bottomed boats – the forerunners of today's punts. The area is based around the Wash and centres on Ely, the area's largest island. Ely is justly famous for its most remarkable Cathedral. There are other abbeys at Ramsey, Thorney, Chatteris, remains of an abbey at Crowland, and there is a priory at Spalding. Fenland stretches away to the north and east of Ely with main ports at Boston and King's Lynn, but Wisbech, 12 miles inland, is also still an active port. Both Wisbech and Spalding were once situated on the medieval coastline of the Wash. Now, after drainage and reclamation, this coastline is very different. Market towns include March, Chatteris, Littleport, Whittlesey and Downham Market. Villages include Upwell, Outwell and Stow Bardolph. Some of the old Fens survive in isolated pockets such as Wicken Fen, which is a protected environment. It was the first National Nature Reserve in England.

FEN HISTORY

Since Roman times the Fens have been a land of tufts of solid ground rising above shallow water, reed beds, pools and mires supporting a vast variety of birdlife. In 1125, the monk William of Malmesbury wrote, 'Here is such a quantity of fish as to cause astonishment in strangers while the natives laugh at their surprise.' The natives in those medieval times enjoyed a steady economy, based on harvesting reeds, peat and rushes.

The drainage of these lands was a project that was taken in hand by Francis Russell, the Earl of Bedford, in 1626. The Earl gathered together a group of investors and called in Dutch engineer Cornelius Vermuyden to drain the Hatfield Chase.

Vermuyden devised a series of ditches (cuts) and dykes and gradually reclaimed the rich peat soil that lay beneath the waters. He was violently opposed by the 'Fen Tigers' (as the more aggressive natives were known), who attacked his workers because he used Dutch workers and changes in the draining had an adverse effect on the locals' traditional hunting and fishing rights. An agreement was reached to compensate the fen-dwellers and to employ English workers, which meant that the project could proceed. Vermuyden worked out a scheme to drain the Great Fen and was promised 96,000 acres for himself as a reward. This work was undone in 1642 when a Parliamentary army broke the Dutchman's dykes in an effort to flood the land and so halt the progress of a Royalist army. In 1649, Vermuyden returned to work with labour provided by Scottish and Dutch prisoners of war. The Great Fen reclamation drained over 40,000 acres of land but caused neighbouring farmland to sink. Peat topsoil dried out and settled, in some cases land sank up to 20 feet below the level of the cuts. Ely's isolation, however, was finally ended.

ELY – ISLAND OF MYSTERIES

It has been said that Ely is an ancient island of mists and tides, a place of eerie enchantment, uninviting and inhospitable yet strangely compelling. Its name means Isle of Eels, after the eels that swam in the waters surrounding the city. As well as providing food the eels were also used as currency. Rents, debts and tithes were often settled by a payment in eels. Ely rose out of its obscurity in the seventh century when St Etheldreda, a Saxon Queen, founded a religious community and a Cathedral on its hilltop site. Ely Cathedral was one of the premier Saxon churches in England, on a par with Glastonbury and Canterbury. The island had been gifted to her by her former husband, Prince Tondbert, Prince of the Fens. Tondbert died of fen-ague (a shivering disease carried by mosquitoes) a few years after the unconsummated marriage. In the eleventh century, Ely was used as a staging post for the Anglo-Saxons, led by Hereward the Wake, in their last stand against the Norman invaders. The island's isolation proved to be useful for the rebels. Inevitably the Normans closed in on Ely but Hereward escaped from here in 1071. He continued to fight on and lived to become a legend. Some historians believe that Hereward was finally defeated in the struggle against superior Norman forces while others hold the view that he was bribed to stop his campaign. The Normans rebuilt Ely Cathedral in 1082 and in 1087 conducted the Domesday survey which recorded, amongst many other facts, that 52,000 eels were caught in the River Ouse (which runs through Ely) in a single year. In the fourteenth century, Alan of Walsingham created the Cathedral's octagonal tower, one of the most amazing feats of engineering in the Middle Ages.

In 1536, an Act of Parliament dissolved smaller monasteries; the rest were induced to surrender individually to royal commissioners during 1537–40. Henry VIII had broken with the Roman Catholic Church and made himself head of a reformed Protestant Church. Bishop Goodrich of Ely complied with the King's orders and his men destroyed sacred shrines and statues, disposed of the saints' bodies and deprived the Benedictine monks of their livelihood.

THE GHOSTLY MONKS OF ELY

After such traumatic events it is perhaps not so surprising that the Cathedral and surrounding grounds at Ely is haunted by monks. In July 2001, the *Ely Standard* interviewed street cleaner Richard Whitehand, who told a reporter about an eerie encounter he had while emptying the refuse bin behind the Goldsmith's Tower. He said, 'I felt a cold chill and looked up to see two monks in cassocks – one was wearing a brown one and one a black – coming through the gate of the Cathedral. I was so scared I dropped everything and froze on the spot. I thought at first someone was mucking about!' The monks crossed the grass and passed through a doorway into the north transept of the Cathedral. Some thirty minutes later they were sighted again as they returned through the arched gateway by the public toilets and turned right behind the Lady Chapel. Mr Whitehand got in touch with the Very Revd Doctor Michael Higgins, Dean of Ely at the time of the incident. Dr Higgins advice was to speak to the apparitions if he came across them again. The next week Mr Whitehand did, indeed, meet the phantom monks again. One afternoon, in the same locality they reappeared, so the street cleaner greeted them by saying, 'Hello, are you alright?' As ghosts usually do, they ignored him and followed their customary path.

Ten years prior to the Whitehand sighting, when Ely Museum was situated in the same vicinity, there was another mysterious occurrence. One winter's morning museum attendant Liz Nardone unlocked the building's back door. She was puzzled to see, to the left of the museum door, facing the blank wall, some oval-shaped footprints in the fresh snow. Liz later remarked, 'I looked up to see if anything was dripping that might have caused the marks, but there wasn't. Then I tiptoed around the yard to see if any footprints led in from the back gate but it was locked and the snow was smooth. The footprints looked like the soles of old fashioned sandals – wider at the toe and narrower at the heel, but without shape and about size six.' The prints certainly matched the general appearance of a sandal from the sixteenth century but no explanation for their unexpected appearance was ever forthcoming.

In the autumn of 1993, Gill Peake saw a ghostly monk when she was working in the Ely Stained Glass Museum, which in those days was located in the gallery above the north transept. Gill had stopped, by the Victorian glass section of the exhibition, to pick up a dropped entry ticket when a movement near the oak doorway caught her attention. She thought at first that it was a woman in a long

Ely Cathedral is haunted by ghostly monks.

swirling coat and an oddly shaped hat. Gill went to the alcove that the figure had seemed to be making for, but the space was empty. The doorway was still in view so no-one could have left that way without being seen. Suddenly there was an extreme temperature drop; at the same time Gill realised that the visitor was not a woman at all. The all-too-solid-looking figure had been that of a Benedictine monk; the 'swirling coat' was his habit and the 'hat' was his cowl. This was Gill's second ghostly encounter; her first had been in February 1989. She was outside the Cathedral this time, on the south side, and it was dusk. She saw Canon Bawtree strolling out of Oyster Lane with his arthritic collie dog dawdling behind; she knew the pair well. Gill said, 'He was walking in the familiar way with his hands behind him, holding the lead.' When she next looked around both man and dog had completely vanished. Cathedral Canon Bawtree had died in November 1988, three months earlier, and his dog had died the previous year …

Novelist Elizabeth Goudge lived at the Deanery in Firmary Lane when she was growing up during the Victorian era, close by the Cathedral. Her father was the Revd Henry Leighton Goudge, Cathedral Canon and principal of the Theological College. Elizabeth wrote in her autobiography about the ghostly guest who would appear by her bed at night. 'He was not a frequent visitor. Nor is he now. For I was not alone in seeing that ghost. Subsequent dwellers in the house have seen him too. I do not know how he appeared to them but to me he appeared as a grey-cowled monk with no face. Where his face should have been there was only darkness. He was not a pleasant person, not like the angel figure who haunted the next door house but one.' The house that Elizabeth referred to was the Black Hostelry, home to Canon Glazebrook and his family. The 'angel figure' ghost certainly scared some visitors, 'for it appeared in the spare room and guests from the outside world were not acclimatised to the unexplainable as we were who lived always in the shadow of history and legend.' A guest saw the figure standing opposite her bed and summoned the old housemaid with a pull of her bedside bell rope. The servant told the guest, 'Why that's nothing to be afraid of I can see it in my room too and I call it my angel. When the moonlight leaves the wall it will go.' In the nineteenth century, Canonry House became a boarding house for King's Girls' School. Some of the boarders reported seeing 'the angel'. She was described as a fair, barefoot girl in a long, white gown, who occasionally haunted a first-floor doorway late at night. It has been surmised that this may have been the ghost of Mistress Pamply, daughter of a headmaster who was dismissed in 1609 for besmirching the establishment's reputation, and his daughter, far from being 'an angel', was said to be 'loose living'.

Elizabeth Goudge mentioned other haunted houses in Firmary Lane. The Black Hostelry, which had formerly housed visiting Benedictine monks, was home to 'something nasty' and Elizabeth knew of at least one guest who had fled the building in terror. The clerical family who lived in Walsingham House (now the

King's School Choir House) were 'weighed down with a sense of misery in a certain part of the house'.

Powcher's Hall was not mentioned by Elizabeth, but it is also located in Firmary Lane and it, too, was haunted by a monk. In 1947, Canon Ratcliff was Professor of Divinity and living at Powcher's Hall. His housekeeper's daughter, Margaret, once encountered a monk in her bedroom. He was dressed in a white habit and he spoke to her in a strange language (possibly Latin). On another occasion the housekeeper herself, while in the garden hanging out some washing, saw a grinning monk appear at a small window beside the back door. She thought that the Canon had an unexpected guest but when she went inside she discovered that her employer was quite alone. The household at Powcher's Hall, including the professor, heard unexplained light footsteps walking along the upstairs corridor, then the drawing room door opening and shutting on occasion. When the professor was away Margaret's grandmother came to stay. One night, loud noises emanating from the haunted top floor were heard by all three female residents. They were too frightened to investigate but in the morning they ventured upstairs together. Instead of finding a disordered mess everything was as they had left it. Canon Ratcliff left Ely in 1958. His housekeeper and her daughter joined him at Cambridge, where he took up the post of Regius Professor of Divinity.

AN ASSORTMENT OF ELY APPARITIONS

Monks are not the only ghosts to inhabit Ely, a variety of manifestations have been recorded in the town over the years. One famous Ely phenomenon is the ghostly hand of St Etheldreda.

In 1539, during the Dissolution of the Monasteries, St Etheldreda's left hand was smuggled out of the Fens, probably hidden in a monk's robes. The sacred relic remained hidden for nearly 300 years until, in the early 1800s, it was rediscovered. The 11th Duke of Norfolk found a reliquary containing the saint's hand. The Duke was in the process of reconstructing his home at Arundel Castle in Sussex at the time. In an estate farmhouse a wall containing a priest's hole was demolished to reveal the hidden reliquary. It was fitted on a silver spike rising from a circular plate of silver inscribed '*Manus Scae Etheldreda 679*'. The spike and plate were contained in a bell-shaped ivory case on an ebony stand with ivory ball supports. The Dukes of Norfolk had been heads of the Roman Catholic Church in England and so the saint's hand had been entrusted to their safekeeping. Charles Howard, the 11th Duke, was a convert to the Anglican Church (the 12th Duke returned to the Roman Catholic faith), so he gave the relic to his estate agent, Mr Harting, who was a Catholic. The agent's son passed the hand on to his daughter, a nun at St Dominic's Priory in Stone, Staffordshire. In 1953, the ancient (over 1,300 years old) well-travelled hand finally arrived home when it was given to Father

Guy Pritchard of St Etheldreda's church in Ely. It was given to him by his sister, who was the chauffeur at St Dominic's Priory. With the arrival of the saint's hand a poltergeist, which had been infesting Father Pritchard's presbytery, suddenly departed. The hand was described as bluish-white at the time but since then exposure has turned it brown.

On a summer night in 1995 three King's School lads caught a fright. They watched, in fascination, as a ghostly, luminous blue hand glided steadily up the back staircase banister. It headed towards them as they prepared for sleep in their dormitory situated in the Priory House Tower.

Ely Cathedral is a truly outstanding edifice, sometimes called 'the Ship of the Fens' because it seems to float across the landscape and, in good weather, it is clearly visible from many miles away. It is justly famous for its Norman stone sculpture and wood carvings as well as its rich wooden Gothic carving in the choir. An interesting account found in the Ely Cathedral archives, 1322–23, tells of the collapse of the Cathedral's Norman tower following the earthquake on 12 February 1322, which exposed the entire Norman Crossing Tower to the elements. A new central tower was designed that seemed to float unsupported above the crossing of Ely Cathedral 'like a cloud' – this was the Lantern Tower. It was a remarkable feat of medieval engineering, formed by massive oak beams rising to a height in excess of 60 feet. Suitable timber was found on the Chicksands Priory estate (the most haunted house in Bedfordshire – see *Paranormal Bedfordshire*). The Great Ouse was Ely's first highway and the massive oak timbers from Chicksands were floated from Bedfordshire all the way to Ely.

Broad Street was Ely's first landward thoroughfare; it runs parallel to the River Great Ouse. The apparition of a woman, dressed in Victorian clothing, has been regularly reported walking along Broad Street towards St Peter's chapel. It is thought that this may be the ghost of Mrs Catherine Sparke, who paid for the construction of St Peter's Chapel of Ease, which was built in 1889. Mrs Sparke commissioned the building in commemoration of her deceased husband, Canon Edward Bowyer Sparke. In January 1994 a mysterious voice was heard, shouting for help. It seemed to come from the vicinity of St Peter's church (which is also situated in Broad Street). A fireman, who lived nearby, answered the vocal distress call but though he searched the area carefully he found no trace of anyone in difficulty. Two months later he had exactly the same experience: once again there was nothing discovered and no explanation was found to account for the disembodied voice.

'Old soldiers never die, they only fade away' and as if to prove the point some old soldiers continue to haunt the Silver Street area of Ely. One particular Non-Commissioned Officer marches the length of Silver Street and turns smartly left into Parade Lane before fading away. This ramrod-straight Sergeant-Major proudly wears his distinctive scarlet jacket decorated with campaign medals and makes his way to the site of the old parade ground (now a car park). This is believed to be the ghost of a military man from the time of George III. Scottish Sergeant-Major John Kyle lived very near to Silver Street, enlisted in 1793 and served in various theatres of war with the Duke of Wellington. In 1802, he became Sergeant-Major of Cambridge Militia, based at Ely. It was his job to put raw recruits from the town and its surrounding villages through three weeks of intensive training every spring. He retired from the army in 1852. During John Kyle's time in Ely the permanent military staff lived in the area bounded by Silver Street, Parade Lane (called Smock Mill Alley then) and the Range (known as the Barracks at that time). In their fascinating book, *Haunted Ely*, Margaret Haynes and Vivienne Doughty chronicle the supernatural history of the town. A haunted cottage in the Range features in a story from the 1970s. A lady had recently moved into her new home when she awoke early one morning to find a strange woman standing by her bed. The stranger was described as 'handsome, healthy-looking, in her late thirties, with lots of black hair'. She 'looked Irish' and wore a 'dazzlingly white apron'. This vision appeared perfectly solid but there was also a 'smaller, fainter soldier'. Behind this ghostly couple 'three or four shadowy children peeped around the door'. It was around dawn and the house was securely locked so they could not possibly be intruders. The apparitions were there briefly and then they were gone.

Silver Street Cottages, Ely: the haunt of Sergeant-Major John Kyle.

The lady lived in her home for ten years but never saw the ghostly family again. Some years later Cathedral guide Christine Pownall researched the history of this cottage as she had moved in next door and heard the story of the haunting. The census of 1881 revealed that Sergeant Atkins and his wife Emma, from County Limerick, had lived in the house. The Atkins family included eight children at the time; Emma was thirty-five years of age. Later on male triplets were born so that there were eleven mouths to feed. Tragedy visited the sergeant and his wife when their two-year-old daughter, Mary Maud, drowned in the wash tub in the back yard. Did this traumatic event cause Emma Atkins' ghost to revisit her former home?

OLIVER CROMWELL

Cambridgeshire's most famous soldier was cavalry commander Oliver Cromwell, who fought in the English Civil War for the Parliamentarians against King Charles I. When war broke out in 1642, Captain Cromwell raised a troop of cavalry from Cambridge and Huntingdon. He led these men at the initial, inconclusive, battle of Edgehill. In 1643, he was promoted to Colonel and expanded his force into a double regiment of horse. This force later became known as the 'Ironsides', combining high morale and rigid discipline with strict morality. In 1644 Cromwell was appointed Lieutenant-General and that July he commanded the cavalry on the left wing of the Parliamentary Army at the battle of Marston Moor. Cromwell and his troopers' valiant charges turned the conflict in favour of the Parliamentarians and inflicted the first major defeat on the Royalist enemy. In 1645 the New Model Army was created under the command of Sir Thomas Fairfax. With discipline, sound training, standardised equipment, a professional approach and a strong religious ethic this army was to prove invincible. Cromwell was made second in command of the force and led his cavalry on the right wing of the New Model Army at the battle of Naseby. Once again the 'Ironsides' distinguished themselves in the struggle and were the decisive factor in the Parliamentarians' victory. In 1646 Cromwell took part in the final stages of the Siege of Oxford, which was the headquarters of the Royalist cause. This presaged the end of the first Civil War. Cromwell returned to London and his career as Member of Parliament for Huntingdon. He worked hard as a conciliator for a constitutional settlement with a king who proved to be both intransigent and deceitful. In 1648 another Royalist uprising, in association with the Scots, meant that Cromwell had to take up arms again, this time as Commander-in-Chief, during this Second Civil War. In July the new Commander-in-Chief quelled the Welsh insurrection at Pembroke Castle. In August he attacked the Royalists at Preston in Yorkshire and broke them. He then moved immediately against the Scots near Warrington and virtually annihilated them at Winwich Pass. Sometimes outnumbered, but never outfought, he had conducted a lightning campaign that wiped out his foes piecemeal; it was a stunning tactical masterpiece. In December 1648 he returned to London and was instrumental in forcing the trial and execution of Charles I in January 1649. In May 1650, however, the Scottish Covenanters proclaimed Charles II to be King. Cromwell returned to England from Ireland, where, as Lieutenant-Governor, he had been successfully waging war on the many Royalist sympathisers there. He led his army into Scotland in July and in September they engaged the enemy. At Doon Hill, near Dunbar, he comprehensively defeated the Scots, under Leslie, who suffered 3,000 dead and 10,000 captured. After a bout of malaria Cromwell returned to the fray in June 1651 and he was to secure his final, crowning victory at Worcester on August 22. His personally led counter-charge, cutting off the Scots break out to the east, sealed their fate. The Prince of Wales (later to become King Charles II), who had been at Worcester, was forced to flee to the Continent. The battle of Worcester ended the Civil War and united the three kingdoms of England, Scotland and Ireland. From the end of 1651 Oliver Cromwell was the *de facto* master of England. In 1653 he dissolved the Rump of the Long Parliament and a Protectorate was established with Cromwell in control of the country as Lord Protector. In 1657 he was offered the crown but refused the offer to be made king. He had never sought greatness; it had been thrust upon him. He did not believe that it was God's will that the monarchy should be restored in the person of King Oliver I. He died in London on 3 September 1658, the anniversary of the battles of both Dunbar and Worcester.

OLIVER CROMWELL'S HAUNTED HOUSE

Oliver Cromwell's former Ely home, which he owned from 1636 to 1647, was originally built in the thirteenth century. It is situated in St Mary's Street and it is now Ely's Tourist Information Centre – with a long-held notoriety as a haunted house. My friends at Cambridge Paranormal Research Society decided to put the place to the test. The team heard reports that in the past a couple of journalists had tried to stay at the house overnight in an attempt to witness firsthand the reputed stories of the ghosts alleged to haunt the museum. The pressmen were said to have fled the house before the night had ended. The CPRS rose to the challenge and after their application to conduct some research was accepted they began their overnight investigation. On Friday 7 November 2003, the CPRS team arrived, at 8.30 p.m. Nothing was left to chance. They had brought a full complement of electronic equipment to test and measure their environment. Three recording and monitoring stations were set up in different locations. Readings were taken for temperature, humidity, air pressure and electromagnetic fields to act as baseline readings for any environmental changes that might occur during the night. Infrared closed circuit television cameras were set up in the haunted bedroom and the study.

Oliver Cromwell's house, Ely. Does the Lord Protector's presence linger here?

They were linked up to motion sensing and recording equipment. Another infrared CCTV was set up in the parlour; it was linked to recording equipment only. Trigger objects were placed in various positions throughout the building and were regularly checked for any possible movement. The team comprised five members – Martin, Elaine, Paul, Dave and Angela. They split into two observation groups: Martin and Elaine in one and Paul, Dave and Angela in the other. The vigil lasted until four o'clock the next morning but it was generally a quiet one, with little to observe or record. This is often the way with paranormal investigation. It is not for the faint-hearted; it requires patience and persistence as hauntings are frequently intermittent and several visits to a site may be necessary before anything of note is witnessed. There were several indications, however, that the house's reputation was justified. In the parlour one of the camera batteries died despite being fully charged. In the Exhibition Room a significant cold spot was felt by two members of the team. A point of light was also observed; it moved from between a mirror on one side of the room and a drum in a glass cabinet on the other side of the room. In the study the thermal temperature gauge inexplicably malfunctioned and in the Haunted Bedroom one of the team felt a pressure on her collarbone. At the conclusion of the night's research it was summed up as a 'strangely quiet' investigation, to quote the CPRS. They further observed, 'Scientific reasoning would have us believe that the expectation of a haunting would in fact produce paranormal phenomena. It is worth noting that one of the members of staff who opened the museum the next morning after we left commented on how quiet and calm the place felt in comparison to other days.'

The CPRS remained intrigued by the atmospheric former home of the Lord Protector. They determined to reinvestigate it, and this time they would also bring along a well-respected psychic medium, the late Marjory Kite, to measure what couldn't be seen or heard by the group's instruments. Martin Waldock and his team returned the following Friday 14 November at 7.30 p.m. to spend another hour at the house. In order to rule out any possibility of their medium conducting research on the place to be investigated the CPRS made sure that Marjorie Kite had no prior knowledge of the location that she would be visiting. To keep the location secret they collected Marjory and took her there themselves. On arrival Marjory immediately picked up impressions. She felt that there was psychical activity in the house. The medium asked if the building had ever been used as a hotel because she had the impression that there would have been many people here at one time. (Research later revealed that the house had been used as an inn, called the Cromwell Arms, between 1843 and 1869.) Marjorie was then taken down to the kitchen. Her intuition was that the room would at one time have been much larger and would have extended back further. She also sensed the presence of a man and described him as a priest, a monk, wearing a long, heavy, grey woollen habit. At one time there would have been many monks in that area, before the Reformation, and they would have been Benedictines. She was given the surname of Roberts. The spirit that she was communicating with was not very helpful – at one time he told her that she was a nosey parker for asking so many questions! (The CPRS learnt that the current kitchen would originally have extended further back, towards the rear car park area. There were Benedictine monks in Ely and they would, typically, have worn heavy woollen robes.)

The most dramatic event occurred in the study, where Cromwell is depicted sitting behind his writing desk. Everyone noticed how cold this room felt. Marjory Kite sat in a chair by the fireplace and said that she could feel activity in here. She asked if some papers had been found behind the fireplace. The man she was sensing was pleased that they had been found, as they were important. This man was against the controlling aspect of the Church. He had needed to break the power of the Church so that ordinary people could think for themselves. The medium had been sitting quietly in the chair when she suddenly began speaking in a loud, strong-sounding male voice. The following statement was given with little hesitation:

How can you fight the establishment? The poor people never stood a chance. That's what made me fight the fight, to release them from bondage. In this day you can think and act as you wish, in my day if you did not believe and attend church you were an outcast. The house was very important to me. My family was very important to me. Unfortunately I did not give them my time. I left them for many months. I am glad you have made this into a museum. You have pleased me very much by what you have done.

Marjory then came out of her trance state, after a few minutes she asked to leave the room as the transfiguration had left her feeling extremely tired. The Tourist Centre manager confirmed that papers had been found behind panelling near a fireplace but in the Tithe Room. The papers were only about 100 years old and have no connection with Cromwell. As a Puritan, Cromwell was strongly opposed to the Roman Catholic religion, which was practised by the Stuart Monarchy. I would agree that he was most probably a loving and caring husband and father (he had nine children). During his Civil War campaigns he was certainly away for months at a time. These circumstances could, however, equally apply to many soldiers in the Parliamentary forces, not just to Cromwell. The statement made by the medium/Cromwell is far too general to be considered as any kind of evidence that it came from this particular man. Marjory Kite later explained that the man she identified as Cromwell, was a kind soul and that she had given him permission to speak through her. Did the voice of Cromwell speak through the medium that night? I don't think so. As an amateur historian, the one word that I would never consider using to describe the Lord Protector would be 'kind'.

Further evidence to justify the haunted reputation of Oliver Cromwell's house was provided in the pages of *Haunted Ely* by Margaret Haynes and Vivienne Doughty. In 2002 Liz Jordan, who worked at the house, told the authors about her encounters with the other-worldly. Liz said, 'As I opened the kitchen door, I saw the bottom half of a person in a long, blue skirt disappearing into a mist by the wall near the fireplace. I shrugged it off as my imagination but then went on a ghost walk around Ely on the following Friday night. When we reached Oliver Cromwell's house, the guide mentioned a blue lady. *I did not know about her* – but at that point, realised I'd seen her.' Could this be the troubled spirit of Cromwell's favourite daughter, who, at just twenty-nine years old, predeceased her father by a matter of weeks? It was said that after her untimely death he 'fell into a distraction of sorrow and then seemed to go under with the sickness himself'. In 1998, Liz Jordan heard a ghost. She was working early one morning at her desk in the upstairs office when she heard heavy footsteps crossing the landing. She assumed that it was Jason, her supervisor, but it was another twenty minutes until he arrived …

The local press, the *Ely Standard*, picked up another report of a haunting in the Cromwell house in December 1998. The previous month, staff at the Tourist Centre saw a grey figure in one of the bedrooms. The December story is the only case that I know of where a ghost is alleged to have untied someone's shoelaces.

Chris Jones was a sceptic when it came to the paranormal. He was employed as an Ely guide for East Cambridgeshire District Council. One day Chris was working in Cromwell's former home, at the back of the building, in what was believed to be a larder or pantry in the past. As he sat at his desk he felt what he described as a strong draught/breeze on his trouser legs. He looked down to find that his left shoelace was untied. He retied it and checked that his other shoelace was securely tied. A few minutes later the breeze returned and this time when he looked down his right shoelace was untied. He shrugged off the incident and carried on with his work until he felt the draught yet again. He checked and saw that his left shoelace was untied for a second time.

Chris said later, 'I really did not believe in ghosts and I am very level-headed but this was really strange. After it happened for a third time I left the room and one of the staff thought something must have been up because they said I looked very pale. I really cannot explain why it happened because there is no practical reason. The laces were tied properly. It is very hard to explain the draught. It was like something gently brushing my leg. Nothing like this has ever happened to me before and since it occurred I have been doing a bit of research into it.' A few days after Chris Jones' experience another male member of staff saw an apparition. He thought that the upstairs part of the building was empty, but on checking he came across what he took to be a visitor in a bedroom. He apologised and told the 'visitor' that the centre was about to close. When the staff member returned downstairs to reception he was told by a colleague that there was nobody left in the house. Together they checked upstairs once more but there was no trace of the 'visitor'. It would not surprise me if Oliver Cromwell haunted his former residence. In life he was an angry man, both ruthless and religious, a visionary and a tortured soul. Such strong emotions may have bound his spirit to earth long after his physical death.

CHAPTER SIX

More Tales from the Fens

WICKEN FEN

Wicken Fen, largely unchanged since Hereward the Wake's time, is probably Cambridgeshire's most iconic haunted location; a wild, unfrequented area, not unlike Dartmoor in Devon. Like Dartmoor it shares the legend of the spectral 'Black Dog', popularised in Victorian times by Sir Arthur Conan Doyle in his novel *The Hound of the Baskervilles*. The creator of Sherlock Holmes had heard accounts of real-life encounters with Black Dogs from around Britain. In East Anglia the local name for this supernatural beast is Black Shuck. Wicken Fen isn't just home to one paranormal legend; it is also infamous as the haunt of the other-worldly 'Lantern Men' as well as a ghostly Roman legion and phantom monks. Wicken Fen is now a 600-acre nature reserve, owned by the National Trust. It is an undrained remnant of the Great Fen of East Anglia, which once covered no less than 2,500 square miles! For hundreds of years the 'Lantern Men' were treated with superstitious awe by those who lived in the Fens. These unexplained lights darted over the top of the marshes and they were believed to be trying to lead the unwary, lost travellers to a watery grave in the flooded reed beds. Strangers were warned not to whistle as dusk fell since the 'Lantern Men' were attracted to the sound of whistling. We now know that the strange, flickering lights are the result of nothing more sinister than marsh gas. The Latin name (which gives some idea of their antiquity) for such lights is *ignis fatuus*, foolish fire. They are usually seen in the vicinity of marshes and churchyards and have also been called 'Will-o'-the-Wisp' and 'Jack-a-Lantern'. The luminosity is caused by the spontaneous combustion of decomposed vegetable matter.

Black Shuck, however, is harder to explain away. Throughout East Anglia it has gained in notoriety over the centuries as the Galleytrot, Old Snarleyow, and Old Scarfe, but most commonly as Black Shuck. Its strong connections to East Anglia in general and Wicken Fen in particular have been largely the result of the numerous well documented cases collected by J. Wentworth Day, country squire and author of *Here Are Ghosts and Witches*. In the 1950s Wentworth Day enjoyed his sport of duck hunting and one night, after a shoot in Wicken Fen, he found himself in a local

Wicken Fen is haunted by Roman soldiers, the 'Lantern Men', 'Black Shuck' and a phantom monk.

inn. The squire invited any of his companions to join him on the walk back home, along an old causeway that had been raised in Saxon times. Nobody accepted the offer and one old countryman told him, 'That owd Black Dog run there o' nights, master. Do ye goo, he'll have ye as sure as harvest.' Fred, an old man who had taught Wentworth Day fishing and shooting skills, also refused and warned that his sister had seen the Black Dog and managed to run away from it. She said that it was 'as big as a calf, moved silently and its eyes were as red as blood ...' This 'hell hound' probably owes its origins to the Norsemen, those raiders who plundered East Anglia, as this was the dog of their All-Father, the Vikings' God, Odin.

Roman soldiers have been sighted in Wicken Fen, appearing briefly before disappearing again as mysteriously as they manifested. Regular reports of them have been received: sometimes marching legionaries are seen, at other times these ancient soldiers have been witnessed fighting noisy battles. What is known is that the Romans did carve out a canal transport route from Lincolnshire through the Fens. It was created to link the fertile lands of East Anglia with the Romans' territories in the Midlands. The Fens would have provided a natural refuge for rebel forces so it is perfectly possible that minor skirmishes could have been fought here.

SPINNEY ABBEY

The 'King of the Ghost Hunters', Peter Underwood, investigated reports of phantom monks in 1971 at Spinney Abbey, which is only a mile from Wicken Fen. Underwood found that Spinney Abbey was 'an isolated collection of buildings grouped round an imposing farmhouse'. Situated on the Stretham Road between Soham Mere and the preserved wetlands of Wicken Fen, Spinney Abbey is a Georgian farmhouse, which offered bed and breakfast facilities to travellers who visit this remote area. I suspect that many would-be ghost hunters may be hoping to spend a night here, given its haunted history. An ancient priory formerly existed on the site and for fourteen years Henry Cromwell, one of Oliver Cromwell's sons, lived at Spinney Abbey and farmed the land. At the time of Peter Underwood's visit the family in residence were the Fullers. Mysterious twinkling lights, reminiscent of the 'Lantern Men', were often seen between the house and Spinney Bank, about a mile away. Local people would go a long way round to avoid Spinney Bank at night. These lights were observed within a hundred yards of the abbey. One local man saw a light move from nearby to illuminate a mill almost a mile away. Nobody ever got really close to the lights because as soon as they were approached they moved further off. When the witnesses stopped the lights appeared to stop too.

Tom Fuller told the ghost hunter that he had seen the apparition of a monk gliding slowly along the garden path and disappearing at an angle of the house. The phantom friar's hood obscured its face. Other people have reported seeing this spectral monk. Unexplained slow, measured footsteps have been heard in the otherwise quiet and peaceful house. One Sunday six people, including the three children of old Robert Fuller, heard music, faint but distinct, accompanied by Latin chanting, in the west part of the house. Robert Fuller had heard the same sounds in the stack-yard several years before but they emanated from a point some 14 feet from the ground. 'Clear as a bell,' he described them, 'pure and sweet, all in Latin and just where the old Chapel of the Abbey used to stand.'

The paranormal investigator went into action when night fell, 'I placed delicate thermometers, at strategic spots: in the piggery where the pigs always fought, the place where the chanting had been heard, another spot where an unexplained female figure had been seen on one occasion and finally where the monk walked. Readings were carefully recorded every ten minutes throughout the night. No thermometer showed any abnormality – except one. Each of them was observed to be steadily declining from around 31°F at midnight to 24°F at 6 a.m. But the thermometer placed where the ghost monk walked showed a sudden and inexplicable drop in temperature of seven degrees! This occurred at 2.10 a.m. and was verified by my two companions; yet the other thermometers showed no similar drop. This one was no more exposed than the others and in any case ten

Spinney Abbey, visited by the ghost of a murdered Abbot.

The front of Spinney Abbey.

minutes later this thermometer showed the temperature back to normal and in line with the others. I have thought of many possible explanations but none that I can accept as probable. It is interesting to note that some horses stabled nearby were quiet throughout the night except at the exact time at which this sudden and unexplained drop in temperature occurred. At exactly 2.10 a.m. the horses suddenly made a terrific noise in their stable, kicking their stalls, whinnying and neighing loudly. Gradually they quietened down and by the time the thermometer showed a normal reading at 2.20 a.m. the horses were quiet again. Horses, like cats and dogs, are believed to be supersensitive, so perhaps some shade of a ghost passed near to me that night.'

Peter Underwood was told by Tom Fuller that an abbot had been murdered at the original Spinney Abbey back in the 1400s. It is a matter of record that on 12 May 1403 the Prior, William de Lode, who had served here for thirteen years, was indeed murdered – stabbed to death in the Priory church by two Canons, Catesson and Smyth. A third Canon, named Hall, broke down the door of the Priory Hall where the Prior had sought refuge. The exact motive for this heinous crime remains unknown as does the fate of the assassins. They were found guilty of murder at Cambridge Castle but the Bishop of Ely ordered that his Canons were subject to clerical law and no further record of the incident survived. Did they get away with murder? This is another one of several unsolved mysteries which surround this sorry tale. Did the unavenged ghostly Prior continue to walk in his former Priory – over 500 years later? The creation of a farmstead wiped out almost all traces of the Priory's existence but in 1935 some skeletons were discovered under the house and their positions indicated a non-Christian burial – were these the remains of the missing murderers?

SOHAM

Not far from Wicken Fen is Soham, which made headlines in the local press during February 2007. The Soham Lodge Motel had a problem with an uninvited guest who was heard but never seen. Stationery left in one room would mysteriously be found moved to other rooms. Guests complained about sleeping badly, particularly in room 11 and some of them had refused point blank to sleep in this room. A cleaner was frightened when she heard someone following her down the corridor and a whispering noise but when she turned around she found herself alone. Other staff saw a clock 'jump off a wall', seemingly of its own accord. The cages which surrounded the bar were sometimes violently rattled by an unseen force. Things reached a head when furniture got thrown around and the manageress, Dawn Spence, was splashed with hot water as a hot tap suddenly turned itself on full pressure and soaked the kitchen floor. Dawn called in local medium Jessica Penberth. The manageress was in for a shock. She had expected to be told that she was the unwitting host to a ghost; the medium told her that there were three wandering spirits at large! Jessica claimed that an eighteen-year-old boy had been killed on the road outside the motel some five or six years previously and he was now one of the ghosts haunting the building. There were two others, older men, one who committed suicide and the other who fell ill at the motel and later died in hospital …

TYDD SAINT MARY

The village of Tydd St Mary is situated on the Lincolnshire border some 6 miles north of Wisbech. In the village stands Hannath Hall, a handsome Elizabethan residence which was originally owned by one Richard Sparrow and known as 'Sparrow's Nest' before being bought by Joseph Hannath in 1812. Legend has it that Joseph Hannath's wife died about forty years later and he seems to have been in denial about her passing. The grief stricken man had his deceased wife placed in an open coffin upstairs in one of the north wing bedrooms. The servants were ordered to take meals up there three times a day. This continued for over a month until the late Mrs Hannath was buried under a chestnut tree in the front garden. Joseph died in 1868 and willed the hall to his sister's children but over the course of the years it passed out of the hands of the Hannath family and most recently it has been owned by the Williams family.

Hannath Hall, Tydd St Mary, was investigated by Tony Cornell, who heard unexplained noises.

The Hall became the subject of much speculation in 1957, soon after the arrival of the new tenant, Mr Page, his wife, two children and his mother-in-law. Derek Page was MP for the constituency of Wisbech and the Isle of Ely at the time. The Page family moved to Hannath Hall in August and before long they were aware of strange things occurring in their new home. They heard all manner of unexplained noises including rapping sounds, footsteps, groans, thumps on doors and once a bed received a hefty jolt from some unseen force.

A local journalist picked up the story, contacted the Society for Psychical Research and two experienced investigators arrived at Hannath Hall that November. They were Doctor Alan Gould and Tony Cornell, who were to form a long-term and successful ghost-hunting partnership. They also brought along two friends from the Cambridge University SPR. The investigators interviewed the family members, apart from the two young children. Phenomena had been confined to the top floor and the haunted bedroom, where Mrs Hannath's body had lain for several weeks during Victorian times.

The SPR team examined every inch of the floorboards of the haunted bedroom with a magnifying glass. They found that they were tongue-and-grooved together. There were no tool marks or splintering detected and they were convinced that no floorboards had been taken up. Next, the ceiling of the room below was likewise examined and the possibility of hidden rapping machinery was thereby excluded. The team measured the whole house, the interior as well as the exterior, to eliminate the possibility of any hiding place for a practical joker.

The vigil at Hannath Hall began around midnight, after the investigators synchronised their watches. Dr Gould was stationed upstairs in the gallery while everyone else was downstairs conducting a séance. Soon after midnight he heard a sharp snap from the haunted bedroom followed, a couple of minutes later, by soft footsteps on the stairs, which stopped before they reached the gallery. Dr Gould went to the head of the staircase but there was no-one on the stairs. At 12.32 a.m. he left his post and went downstairs because it had become so cold in the gallery. The temperature had plummeted from 60°F to 52°F. At 1.25 a.m. Alan Gould and Tony Cornell returned upstairs; they had decided to spend the rest of the night in the haunted bedroom. It was used as a storeroom for unwanted furniture and it had no electricity. The investigators settled down for an uncomfortable night on two mattresses, end to end, with a single blanket over their legs to ward off the cold. The temperature sank to 49°F and remained there for some time. Minutes after switching off their torches they both heard gentle taps coming from the floor. The investigators found that a specific number of raps could be produced on request. They got louder and moved nearer to the wall of the room. The raps would respond in answer to leading questions but couldn't spell out coherent messages. The rapper claimed to be a woman who was murdered in the house in 1906 (but Gould and Cornell were subsequently unable to substantiate this).

After a while a series of six or seven knocks were heard and they got progressively louder. The last one was of such intensity that Gould flashed his torch in its direction. Immediately the knocks ceased, and all that the torch illuminated was bare floorboards. About this time the séance downstairs broke up and Murray and Brotherton, the other members of the CUSPR, came up to the gallery. They too heard the rapping noises and then Mr Brotherton went downstairs again to search the room immediately below the haunted bedroom while Mr Murray stayed outside the door of the haunted room. Brotherton found the Page family sitting round the table in the living room; he then rejoined Murray upstairs and was told that the raps had continued throughout his absence. Both men decided to go downstairs again and search the room immediately below the haunted bedroom. After about ten minutes or so the raps began upstairs again, so Gould and Cornell asked the month of the supposed communicator's death and in response were given eleven raps. They then asked the day of the month and a series of raps moved along the floor until the sixteenth rap seemed to come from thin air, just behind Cornell's head. The raps started to get fainter after this and then ceased altogether, and Gould and Cornell returned downstairs at a quarter to three. At 3.34 a.m. Gould and Cornell returned with Murray. As the door was slammed they all heard a sharp rattle. The three investigators turned, and by torchlight a brass toasting fork with three prongs was seen to have been thrust behind the metal plate to which the door bolt was attached. One of its prongs was inserted through the staple into which the bolt normally ran, thus 'bolting' them into the room from the inside.

All four of the CUSPR men wrote preliminary notes on the phenomena within minutes of their occurrence. These notes were later amplified into fuller statements. The team all heard the raps and agreed that they were in answer to questions. They did not usually occur during the time that they were asking questions and came in an even tempo at a rate of one per second or faster. Immediately after a question was put answering raps would begin. They were appropriate in number to the questions asked, such as one for 'yes' and eleven for November. Once a question received an appropriate answer there was nearly always a silence until the next question was posed.

Gould and Cornell returned for a second visit on 21–22 November 1957 when some more rappings, faint and distant-sounding, were heard. Between them the investigators paid some twenty visits to the house in all. On 25–26 April 1959, they brought along a non-professional medium with them and held a séance in the haunted bedroom. A lady called Eliza Cullen or Culler came through and said that she had made the raps. She said she had buried her baby in the garden, but no trace of any person of that name could be found.

On 22 April 1959 and again in July 1959 Mrs Page, when in the living room, twice reported seeing the figure of a small, fair-haired boy peering at her round the boxroom door when she was certain that there was no-one there.

All of Alan Gould's and Tony Cornell's reports, notes and other documentation on this intriguing case remain in the care of the Society for Psychical Research.

WISBECH

Wisbech is known as the 'Capital of the Fens'. It is a small Georgian market town of great character and the Bowling Green Tap pub in Chase Street is a well-known haunted site. It is frequented by a spirit called 'Charlie', whose apparition is likened to that of a Quaker. This would probably date this apparition to the 1700s, which is when the Quaker faith originated in England. Also known as the Society of Friends, this faith is very different to any other Christian sect in that it doesn't have a universally governing creed. Instead the central guiding principal is that the spirit comes from within, a concept known as 'inner light' which governs a Quaker's beliefs. This faith also holds to the tenet of simple and honest living. The most famous Quaker is Elizabeth Fry, the humanitarian and prison reformer, who was born in 1780. The 'Quaker' who haunts the Bowling Green Tap makes his presence known these days with poltergeist activity and he has been described as mischievous and sometimes quite violent.

Wisbech featured in the pages of the *Eastern Daily Press* in 1965 when paranormal activity was reported from the Continental Shoe Repair Shop at 22 High Street. A staff member, alone in the workroom, had his tools snatched from his hands by some invisible force and soon his workmates were being similarly affected. Other phenomena were experienced, lights would switch themselves on and off and doors would suddenly open for no reason. Overnight, heavy machinery was found to have been moved from its original place. On the staircase leading to the attic, footsteps and the rustle of long skirts was heard. The locked attic had been empty for many years. The *Eastern Daily Press* sent a reporter and photographer to cover the story and they were accompanied by Bill Hyams, the manager of the shop. The trio climbed up to the attic and entered the disused junk room. There on the dusty floor all three men saw a strange sight. The imprint of a woman's left foot crossed the room from the window to the blocked-up fireplace. Some days later Bill Hyams decided to revisit this room and he pulled away the hearth covering to reveal some Victorian women's clothing and a scrapbook. This was witnessed, once again, by the local news reporter. The *Eastern Daily Press* reviewed this strange incident in October 1989, together with Tony Cornell, from the SPR, who had investigated the case. His quote summed up the baffling story: 'The problem was that the things which were said to be going on were seen by only one person at a time … This part of the town is honeycombed with underground passages, running to the river, and they can have the effect of producing some very strange noises at times. At the same time, that does not explain what a bare-footed woman was doing hopping around in an upstairs room.'

An eerie example of EVP (electronic voice phenomena) featured in an issue of *Fortean Times* magazine during 2000. A letter sent in by a Wisbech resident described his paranormal experience. He was pleased after recently purchasing one of the very latest digital telephone answering machines (at that time) with a chip instead of a cassette. One night he missed a call but managed to pick up the receiver just as his caller was leaving a message. He reported, 'Later that evening as I was about to erase the start of that message I picked up what sounded like another voice in the tiny gap between the end of my pre-recorded message and the start of the caller speaking.' Intrigued, the Wisbech man turned the volume up to the maximum and his blood ran cold. The strange voice spoke in a low, menacing way but the words were unintelligible.

TONY CORNELL, PARAPSYCHOLOGIST

Tony Cornell, who was from Cambridgeshire, died in April 2010, aged eighty-six, after spending decades investigating the paranormal. He was born in Histon and educated at the Perse School and Fitzwilliam College then Fitzwilliam House, where he graduated in 1949. During the Second World War, he served in the Black Watch Regiment and was posted to India before volunteering for the Royal Indian Navy. As a naval officer he saw action off Trincomalee, Sri Lanka and in Burma. His interest in the paranormal was initiated by a number of unexplained experiences during his service in India. Married three times, he is survived by three sons. A man of many interests, Tony cared deeply for his home county; as an amateur antiquarian he helped ensure the preservation of timber-framed buildings opposite Cambridge Town's Round Church. In the 1960s, he became a councillor and was chairman of both City and County Planning Committees over a sixteen-year period. Possibly the greatest legacy of Tony Cornell was when his original suggestion that a science park should be built in Cambridge finally became a reality. His proposal was that local councillors and Trinity College should get together to establish what was to become the present site on college land off Milton Road.

For many years the parapsychologist was president of Cambridge University Society for Psychical Research, which met in the basement of his house in Victoria Street. He became an acknowledged authority on the paranormal and was consulted by the media; he published many papers and books. His stated opinion was that he was highly sceptical about the existence of ghosts but kept an open mind. Tony was a thoroughly modern investigator, the man who invented SPIDER (Spontaneous Psycho-physical Incident Data Electronic Recorder) to help him in his investigations. His friend Christopher South, a columnist with the *Cambridge News,* had this to say: 'He had a very surprising attitude. Most people who are interested in the occult or strange events are trying to prove they are real and he spent his whole life proving they weren't. He was very, very difficult to persuade anything strange was going on. He would spend hours of his life in an empty room only to emerge and say nothing happened. He was a very interesting man.' Not a bad epitaph and though I never met him I think I would have shared Christopher South's opinion. A memorial and celebration of Tony Cornell's long and full life was held at Fitzwilliam College in June 2010.

ELM'S ETHEREAL ECHOES

Elm village is situated about two miles south of Wisbech and Elm Vicarage is reputed to be a place where a ghost intervened to save a woman's life. Expert ghost hunter Peter Underwood investigated the case and the story is related in his excellent book, *The A–Z of British Ghosts*. The vicarage was a rambling, 200-year old building, which was haunted by a monk who died over 750 years ago and by a bell that tolled a death-knell. Peter Underwood's contacts were the Revd A. R. Bradshaw and his wife. Mrs Bradshaw would hear the bell and the next day the vicar invariably learned of a death in his parish. This happened no less than thirty-one times in two-and-a-half years. The hauntings began with unexplained footsteps, heard night after night, soon after the Bradshaws moved into Elm Vicarage. The vicar initially went in search of an intruder but was unable to find any normal cause for the footsteps or even an exact location from where they came. The nocturnal footsteps continued until a ghostly monk, Ignatius, appeared. One evening, in an upstairs corridor, Mrs Bradshaw brushed up against the monk, who was wearing a brown habit and sandals. He spoke to her, 'Do be careful', whereupon the vicar's wife asked her uninvited guest who he was. The man replied, 'Ignatius, the bell-ringer'. The vicar's wife subsequently encountered the ghost many times and gradually learned his story. A monastery used to occupy the site of the rectory and this is where Ignatius died more than 700 years ago. One of Ignatius's responsibilities had been to watch the flood waters rising in the nearby Fens and to warn his brothers if there was any danger. One night he was asleep and he did not ring the warning bell when the waters rose to a dangerous level. The monastery was inundated, some monks were drowned and Ignatius was disgraced.

Peter Underwood was intrigued and asked Mrs Bradshaw to describe exactly how Ignatius usually became visible and whether he always appeared at the same spot. She informed the researcher/writer that she had seen the monk in various parts of the house, sometimes in the upstairs corridor where he had first appeared, sometimes in the parlour, and occasionally elsewhere. He first appeared as a fine outline, then gradually emerged into the figure of a man aged about thirty-three with 'dark, curly hair and thin ascetic features'. She usually saw him at dusk and he always wore a brown monk's habit that looked old and worn.

One September night Mrs Bradshaw was going to sleep in a bedroom usually reserved for visitors. Afterwards this room was used as a box room and the door kept securely locked. The family dog invariably slept on Mrs Bradshaw's bed but this night he whimpered and cried and repeatedly ran out of the room. He had to be brought back three times and eventually he was persuaded to stay.

The vicar's wife put out the light and went to sleep. She awakened with a feeling that something was being tied around her neck. She reached for her torch and discovered that a tendril of wisteria from the wall outside the bedroom window had made its way through the open window and lay across her throat. She tore it away and then the bedclothes were pulled from her. Terrified, she felt herself being violently picked up and thrown sideways across the bed. By now speechless with fright, she became aware of a vague black shape looming over her and through what appeared to be a haze, a pair of gnarled hands materialised and clutched at her throat. She tried her hardest to scream but no sound would come. The hands tightened their hold and she had to use every ounce of her willpower to fight the increasing pressure for she found that she was powerless to defend herself physically. Suddenly she saw Ignatius. He came towards her, reached for the twisted hands clutching at her throat and pulled them away. As the pressure on her throat relaxed, Mrs Bradshaw collapsed back on to the bed, totally exhausted. She hardly had time to catch her breath before she became aware of the horrible creature bending over her again. It had a huge head and a red face. The dog was on the bed, snarling and fighting something invisible. Summoning all her remaining strength, the woman tore herself free and rushed into her husband's room. The marks on her throat remained for almost a week. The first her husband knew of the episode was when he was awakened by his wife, but he confirmed to Underwood that her throat was badly bruised and that the marks remained visible for days.

When the vicar's wife next saw Ignatius she asked him who had attacked her and she was told that he was a man who had been murdered in that room. Ignatius later told Mrs Bradshaw that he would not be seeing her so often in the future; having saved her life had gone some way towards completing his penance so he was hopeful of complete forgiveness and rest. Mrs Bradshaw remained convinced that a ghost saved her life that night.

RAMSEY

Situated in the far west of the Fens, the town of Ramsey is reached by a narrow road which travels along the embankment, high above the surrounding land. This causeway-like, narrow, back country road links Ramsey to other neighbouring small and ancient Fen towns like Whittlesey and Thorney.

A drama was played out in sleepy Ramsey in May 2009, when fire broke out in its Grade II listed, 400-year-old hotel, the George, situated in High Street.

George Hotel, Ramsey, is home to a ghost who hates fire.

The blaze caused both guests and hotel staff to be evacuated in the small hours of the morning. The fire, which was blamed on an electrical fault, started in an empty storage room on the top floor of the George Hotel. Strangely the blaze was contained to this one room, known as the 'haunted room' or 'Mary's room'. Was this just coincidence? The ghost that haunts the hotel is believed to be that of a former landlady named Mary. It is believed that she perished from smoke inhalation during a fire in the building long ago. The Axelson family, who own and run this charming establishment, will tell you that the ghost hates fire so much that she has been known to steal people's lighters and to blow out candles. The ghost was also said to be responsible for a variety of poltergeist-like activity. Louis Axelson, the young hotel manageress, has been quoted as saying 'We do not mind Mary, you get used to having her around. If you work here, then you are aware that you are also working with ghosts.'

WITCHFORD

It was back in 1998 when I first came across Lancaster Way Business Park, which is the site of the former bomber station, RAF Witchford, situated some three miles west of Ely. I was delighted to discover in the Business Park the RAF Witchford Display of Memorabilia. Not much of the old bomber station remains – an area of the runways was used for poultry units and the landing ground area has been reclaimed for arable farming. I learned that this Class 'A' standard airfield was built in 1942 and opened for operations in 1943. Its operational lifespan was extremely short; it was closed and broken up in 1946. Vickers Wellingtons from 196 Squadron were based here; they were later replaced by Avro Lancasters of 115 Squadron (due to the Wellington's vulnerability to night defences). I was later to learn that Witchford was haunted. In October 2009, a couple were visiting the site of the old airfield and the husband, who knew the site well, was looking towards where the old runway used to be. Suddenly the pair heard the sound of aero engines and they were aware of the shadowy shapes of people all around them, passing close by in the moonlight (it was about 10.30 p.m.). The couple were conscious of a feeling of great activity but after a few minutes everything returned to normal and all was quiet again.

CHAPTER SEVEN

Supernatural South Cambridgeshire

In the *Best & Worst Places to Live in the UK* feature on Channel 4 in 2006, South Cambridgeshire emerged as the fifth best out of the top ten areas in which to live. Some 434 UK local authorities were judged on exactly the same criteria: crime, education, employment, environment and lifestyle. South Cambridgeshire is an agglomeration of rural villages that entirely surround the City of Cambridge. The summary given to South Cambridgeshire was 'Fast growing country villages'. It is undoubtedly a pleasant place in which to reside – it has, however, another reputation, as home to numerous ghosts and other paranormal phenomena.

CAXTON GIBBET

The A1198 is the modern London to Huntingdon road but it follows the line of a much older Roman road, Ermine Street. The A1198 crosses the current A428, the Oxford to Cambridge road. Close by this crossroads, on a small knoll, stands a replica of a gibbet, known as Caxton Gibbet. A gibbet was an upright post with a projecting arm from which the bodies of criminals were dangled in chains or irons after execution. These gruesome public displays, which could be seen for many months, served as a warning to those who might consider breaking the law in the days when hanging was the punishment for stealing an item worth five shillings or more. Gibbets were in use in the seventeenth and eighteenth centuries. The last documented case of their usage was in the early nineteenth century. The Caxton Gibbet area is steeped in legend and history, and one of the most infamous stories concerns the landlord of an inn that stood at this crossroads during the eighteenth century. He was notorious as a man who was quick to anger, quarrelsome and thoroughly dishonest. Three wealthy travellers stayed the night at his inn and the landlord couldn't resist some easy pickings. While his guests slept, the villain took his chance and rifled the traveller's pockets and baggage. Unfortunately one of the travellers was a light sleeper and challenged the thieving landlord, who then murdered his guest. The other potential witnesses had to die too, so the ruthless innkeeper struck them all down. He solved the problem of disposing of their bodies by the simple expedient of dumping them in the well. His crime was uncovered, however, and he was hanged. The murderer's body ended up in the gibbet that stood close to his inn. Long after this crime the pub continued to be haunted by the former innkeeper's ghostly footsteps. They were heard to cross the balcony, descend to the ground floor and stop at the foot of the stairs. This was near to the well into which the murdered men's bodies had been secreted.

Crossroads are associated with many superstitions and the site of the crossroads at Caxton Gibbet is no exception. The area was described, in 1822, by journalist and reformer William Cobbett as, 'bleak and comfortless'. It is said that the bodies of three men who were executed for stealing sheep are buried at this spot. One of the strangest true stories I heard about the crossroads was an eye-witness account of an apparition seen in fairly recent years. It was dusk and the light was still quite strong as a woman and her husband were driving along the A428 between St Neots and Caxton Gibbet. The man slammed on his brakes when he saw a coach and horses passing from left to right in front of his motor car at the Caxton Gibbet crossroads. Fortunately there was nothing else travelling in their immediate vicinity or an accident might have occurred. The wife later explained that the couple had both plainly seen this conveyance from another age. She recalled that it seemed solid enough at the time, but she was sure it was 'not quite on the actual road'.

DUXFORD

Today Duxford Aerodrome is jointly owned by the Imperial War Museum and Cambridgeshire County Council. It is world famous as the home to the Imperial War Museum and the American Air Museum's unique collection of First and Second World War aircraft. There is also a Land Warfare Museum, which contains many interesting exhibits.

During the First World War, many of the buildings at Duxford were constructed by German prisoners of war. In 1936 Flight Lieutenant Frank Whittle, who was studying at Cambridge University, flew regularly from the aerodrome as a member of the Cambridge University Squadron. Whittle went on to develop the jet turbine and Britain produced the Allies' first open jet fighter in 1943 – the Gloster Meteor. In 1938 Number 19 Squadron became the first to fly the new Supermarine Spitfire and the first Spitfire was flown into Duxford by Jeffrey Quill, Supermarine's chief test pilot.

Nineteen Squadron was to move to nearby Fowlmere, Duxford's satellite station, for the Battle of Britain, which began in June 1940. Hurricanes from 310 Squadron, flown by Czechoslovakian pilots who had escaped from France, arrived in July 1940. September 1940 saw intense air fighting. On 9 September squadrons from Duxford intercepted and turned back a large force of Luftwaffe bombers before they reached their target. This was to prove the importance of Duxford and two more squadrons were added. These were 302 (Polish) Squadron and

611 Auxiliary Squadron, equipped with Spitfires. Acting Squadron Leader Bader was an enthusiastic supporter of the 'Big Wing' tactic, which was proposed by 12 Group Commander Air Vice-Marshall Trafford Leigh-Mallory. The tactic was to meet incoming German aircraft on bombing raids in strength, with wing-sized formations of 3 to 5 squadrons (about thirty–sixty fighters). It had mixed results. An average of sixty Spitfires and Hurricanes were dispersed around Duxford and Fowlmere every day. 15 September was Battle of Britain Day; fighters from Duxford took to the air twice on that day. The Germans now realised that, far from being beaten, the RAF was able to successfully repulse any attack, no matter how large, that the Luftwaffe could send against it. The Germans had lost far too many aircraft and therefore had lost the struggle for air supremacy over Britain.

I have greatly enjoyed the outstanding live air displays and museum exhibits on my outings to Duxford. It was particularly thrilling to be invited to sit inside the rebuilt 'Memphis Bell' Flying Fortress some years ago. There is, however, another dimension to Duxford, one where the paranormal intrudes on the well-ordered life of this fine museum. I have been privileged to dine at the restored Officers' Mess and it has been mentioned that some people feel distinctly uneasy when walking between the hangars and the Officers' Mess. They have reported sensing unseen presences and being watched by these entities. Given the violent end that awaited most RAF fighter pilots who defended our skies between 1939 and 1945 I would be surprised if Duxford and indeed many other Second World War airfields weren't haunted...

In 2003, a ghost-hunting group was given permission to spend the night in the control tower at Duxford – a rare privilege indeed. It was said that some of the team saw a ghostly B-17 American bomber re-enacting a fatal crash at the airfield, a crash that had actually been recorded in the past. There have been a number of other reports, including 'a presence' felt in Hangar 5, and 'a mortally wounded soldier' has been sensed inside the ambulance at the Land Warfare Museum. A Duxford worker said, in 2005, that a workshop near the base mortuary was 'eerie on dark winter evenings' and that he had heard the sounds of slamming doors and footsteps coming from empty hangars. I am fairly confident that these snippets of information are just the tip of a much larger collection of anomalous phenomena that goes largely unrecorded...

GRANTCHESTER

The Old Vicarage at Grantchester is well known as the country home of one of Britain's most successful fiction writers, Lord Jeffrey Archer and his wife Dr Mary Archer. The lovely old house is also famous in its own right. Before Lord Archer acquired the property it was home to one of the country's most revered poets, Rupert Brooke (1887–1915), who died so tragically young at just twenty-eight years of age. A statue of the poet stands in the garden of the Old Vicarage. It was rumoured that the ghost of Rupert Brooke revisited his former home, but Lord Archer has always denied that his house is haunted and his wife is also on record as having had no paranormal experiences while living at Grantchester. What is indisputable is that Rupert Brooke loved his home. Many people know the lines 'Stands the clock at ten to three? And is there honey still for tea?' They are taken from Brooke's poem 'The Old Vicarage, Grantchester'. Ghosts return to haunt the places where they were happiest as well as to places where they suffered great trauma, such as in the case of either suicide or murder. As with George Bernard Shaw (see *Paranormal Hertfordshire*) who seems to have returned to his beloved former home, Shaw's Corner in Ayot St Lawrence, it may be that the shadow of Rupert Brooke has also walked at his former residence.

According to my friend Peter Underwood, some former residents at the Old Vicarage, Mr and Mrs Dudley Ward, were convinced that their home was haunted when they lived there some fifty years ago. Peter writes in *Haunted Gardens* about the Wards' numerous encounters with the otherworldly. These extraordinary experiences included 'unexplained footsteps coming up the garden towards the sitting room' and 'poltergeist activity' occurring in the little ruined summerhouse at the bottom of their garden (where furniture was moved about during the night when the place was unoccupied by any living being). The Wards told Peter Underwood that the disembodied footsteps came from the garden into the sitting room, up the stairs then continued to move about upstairs, accompanied by the sounds of books being moved. The noises from above could last for up to half an hour. Was this the spirit of Rupert Brooke revisiting his former home and sorting through his library? Nor were the Wards the only witnesses to these strange visitations; friends and visitors also heard this unexplained phenomena which could occur at various times, day or night. Shapeless forms were sighted on many occasions in the gardens. Why then is no recent activity reported? Hauntings often fade away with the passage of time, so perhaps this particular site is now free of unseen presences. Alternatively the Archers may not be sensitive to ghostly presences, for while some people are psychically gifted others are decidedly more grounded in the material world.

GUILDEN MORDEN

One of my historian friends, Brian Jones, lives at Market Deeping in Peterborough, but he grew up in the South Cambridgeshire village of Guilden Morden. After two years of patient research, Brian finally unlocked the true story behind his home village's most famous old ghost story. I am delighted to include the accurate version here for the first time. On 20 April 1845, the ship *Cataraqui* sailed from Liverpool bound for Australia. On board were 369 passengers and forty-four crew members. Among the passengers were twenty-three persons from four families, who had left Guilden Morden for a new life abroad. On 4 August, tragedy struck when the ship

St Mary's church at Guilden Morden was the scene of a 'death knell' spontaneously tolled when twenty-three villagers drowned off the Australian coast on 4 August 1845.

hit a reef and sank in the entrance to the Bass Strait. At that exact moment, on that same day, back in far away Guilden Morden, the church bell tolled of its own accord and no-one knew the reason why.

It wasn't until February 1846 that the complete story was revealed by the *Cambridgeshire Chronicle*. The edition of 7 February told the full story (as revealed by a survivor) and the edition of 14 February gave the names of the dead from Guilden Morden. On 15 February 1846, the vicar at Guilden Morden's church preached a sermon based on 'the Resurrection and the Last Judgement' concerning 'the shipwreck of the emigrant ship Cataraqui off King's Island, Bass Straits on 4th August last'.

In the field of paranormal investigation one of my icons is T. C. Lethbridge, whom writer Colin Wilson once described as 'one of the most remarkable and original minds in parapsychology'. T. C. had an extremely interesting paranormal experience at Guilden Morden as a young man of twenty-three. Thomas Charles Lethbridge (1901–71) discovered his interest in archaeology while studying at Cambridge University. He later became Director of Excavations for the Antiquarian Society and for the University Museum of Archaeology, posts he held for thirty years. He became bored with 'academic trade unionism' and retired in 1956 to Hole House, his home in Branscombe, Devon. For the remaining fifteen years of his life, he devoted his time to the scientific research of various paranormal subjects. His factually based theories on occult subjects included dowsing, ghosts, psycho-kinesis and witchcraft. Between 1961 and 1971, he had eight classic works about the supernatural published. Anyone with a serious interest in the paranormal should read them all. As the great man himself said, 'What is magic today will be science tomorrow.'

Lethbridge was part of an archaeological research team at Guilden Morden during the summer of 1924. A Romano-British cemetery was the subject of the team's excavations and Lethbridge noted down a number of frightening anomalous phenomena which surrounded the dig at Guilden Morden. The incidents were covered in one of Lethbridge's books, which was published in the early 1960s called *Ghost And Ghoul*. While reading this I was, once again, transported back to the 1970s and reminded of the comment made by Danny Ward back then (as described in *Paranormal Bedfordshire*), 'If disturbing bodies upsets the dead, who knows what being put on public display will do?' The skeletal remains discovered on site were taken back to Cambridge by motor car and 'gremlins' seemed to be responsible for the high incidence of problems encountered on the journey. (For those too young to have encountered the term, gremlins were mischievous sprites said to be responsible for unexpected mechanical or electrical faults. It was coined during the Second World War amongst RAF ground crew responsible for aircraft maintenance.) Inexplicable brake failures occurred and on one notable day, whilst travelling between Royston and Melbourn at about 30 miles per hour, the nearside front wheel of Lethbridge's car just 'disappeared'. Fortunately an accident was avoided and the car came to a safe stop. The young archaeologist and his passenger had to continue their journey by bus (they were transporting a box of skulls at the time). Later Lethbridge showed his hostess, a Canon's wife, a skeletal finger, still wearing an ancient ring. The lady was obviously shocked, 'How very unlucky' she exclaimed. It certainly was. The very next day this lady suffered a fit and died while doctors tried to resuscitate her. As Lethbridge reminisced, how had those 'boxes of grinning skeletons' influenced events?

LINTON

A charming village on the Cambridge/Essex border, Linton is probably the only English village to boast both a zoo and a vineyard. It was where Britain's answer to Uri Gellar, our own Matthew Manning, spent his formative years. Matthew can do many of the things that Uri has become famous for, such as metal-bending, and much more besides. Matthew has also undergone exhaustive tests by scientists, including members of the Mind Science Foundation in Texas, the University of California, the Los Angeles University and the London University. A visit to the Himalayas in India revealed to Matthew Manning his true destiny – full-time psychic healer.

Cambridge was home to Matthew during his early life and at the tender age of eleven his close link to the world of the paranormal made itself apparent. Classic poltergeist activity invaded the Manning household. Moving house didn't improve the situation. When the Mannings and their three children settled into their seventeenth-century home in Linton in 1968 things remained quiet for a couple of years. Then, in the summer of 1970, the poltergeist phenomena gradually returned, increasing in both frequency and variety so that by the following year a plethora of phenomena had been recorded. These included items stacked or arranged, missing things found in unusual places and the movement of large items. Sixteen-year-old Matthew was to discover that he could now use astral, see auras and produce automatic drawing and writing. A significant turning point came for this young man when he saw a shadowy figure on the staircase of the family home. Looking more closely, it appeared to the developing psychic that the man on the stairs was completely solid. He described the ghost in some detail, 'He was wearing a green frock coat with frilled cuffs and a cream cravat.' Then the ghost spoke, 'I must offer you my most humble apology for giving you so much fright, but I must walk for my blessed legs.' The youngster made a sketch of his visitor on the back of an envelope before the apparition turned, walked up the stairs and disappeared.

Through his newfound powers of automatic writing (when the writer lets his hand and pen be guided by another, unseen presence), Matthew Manning was able to exchange messages with the ghost. He learned a lot. The ghost's name was Robert Webbe, he was born in the house in 1678, and in later life he walked with the aid of two sticks, due to his 'troublesome legs'. Webbe had been a grain trader and he had been most proud of his house, which he enlarged but didn't live long enough to enjoy. He had died in the house in 1733. The ghost wrote messages on the walls of Matthew's bedroom; more than 500 names and dates appeared during a six-day period in July 1971.

Webbe had many other methods of making his presence known. Apports (the spontaneous manifestation of an object or item) from a bygone age would be found on the stairs. The smell of strong pipe tobacco (in a house of non-smokers) was smelt. In Matthew's parents' bedroom the covers would be found thrown back and the pillows dented as though someone had been lying there. Anomalous sounds were heard – heavy footsteps in empty rooms, the noise of a bell ringing in the hallway when there was no bell in the house, and a lit candle was found on the cloakroom floor.

The psychic asked the ghost about the various phenomena and Webbe admitted his responsibility, but said it was *his* house and he could do whatever he wanted in it. When Matthew tried to shake hands with Webbe his hand passed straight through. The psychic said later, 'At that moment I experienced an eerie feeling of timelessness.' Matthew Manning came up with his own theory about the haunting, which was to have such a profound effect on him. 'He wanted to take the house with him. I think that is why he was going round and round in a strange sort of time loop, trapped by his own will in infinity. Then from time to time, someone in the house provided him with enough psychic energy to allow him to make contact.' As interesting a theory as you will find in the annals of ghosts and hauntings. There was an amusing postscript from Matthew Manning, 'I remember asking him during my research into local history why the house was haunted. He replied he did not believe in ghosts – and, in any case, there were none in the house!'

MADINGLEY HALL

In the village of Madingley, some four miles west of Cambridge, lies a Tudor mansion which is owned by Cambridge University. Madingley Hall has been extensively refurbished in recent years and it is presently used as a residential centre for continuing education and conferences. The Hall was built in 1543 by Sir John Hynde, but he didn't enjoy it for long as he died in 1550. His son Sir Francis Hynde had the task of completing the building. Madingley Hall remained in the hands of his descendants until 1871, and then it passed through several other families' ownership before finally being purchased by the university in 1948.

The poet Rupert Brooke (previously mentioned in connection with Grantchester) also wrote the following lines:

> And things are done you'd not believe
> At Madingley on Christmas Eve.

This verse, although pure invention by the poet, might almost refer to the anniversary ghost of Madingley Hall. This is Lady Ursula Hynde, wife of Sir John Hyde, the original owner of the mansion. Her shade has been reported as appearing on the path between the Hall and St Mary Magdalene Church, which is situated just inside the main gate of the estate. The apparition wrings its hands in grief for the misdeeds of Lady Ursula's wayward son Sir Francis. It was Sir Francis who allegedly took the timber and stone from St Etheldreda's church at Histon, a building he had demolished in order to rebuild parts of Madingley Hall. His mother was said to be deeply ashamed about her son's lack of piety.

Lady Ursula is not alone in haunting Madingley Hall. Another eyewitness account tells of a ghostly party of people in Tudor costume. Among them was a particularly unattractive young man, with an evil expression on his face, which was tinged with the green of advanced decay. Some have described his visage as 'skull-like'.

Another ghost seen at Madingley Hall haunts the courtyard. She is thought to be a younger daughter of the Hynde family from the seventeenth century. It is said that her prospective bridegroom died a matter of days before the planned wedding. This tragic young woman, who is alleged to have subsequently died of a broken heart, returns in her bridal gown, walking the courtyard. One story about her sighting is associated

Madingley Hall is where Lady Ursula Hynde haunts her former home.

with the Second World War. It is claimed that the military briefly occupied part of Madingley Hall and one night a sentry challenged 'the phantom bride' and when she didn't respond the soldier opened fire whereupon the vision in white dematerialised.

SAWSTON HALL

Sawston Hall is probably the most famously haunted great house in South Cambridgeshire. Sawston village, situated on the River Cam, seven miles south of Cambridge, is the largest village in this county. The Hall is a Grade I listed stately home which was owned by the Huddleston family for over 460 years. Set in 60 acres of grounds, the Hall was known for its fine Great Hall with Elizabethan panelling, its private chapel with beautiful stained glass windows and its priest's hole, set at the top of the spiral staircase. To remain staunch Catholics in a Protestant country invited persecution and fines. This meant that the Huddlestons kept just enough money to maintain their home but not enough to alter it structurally. The result was that the house remained intact, as a perfect example of a completely original and unspoilt Tudor mansion. The charming home was thrust into the pages of history one night in 1553. Queen Mary I was running for her very life, pursued by the relentless John Dudley, the Duke of Northumberland, who was intent on arresting and imprisoning her. The scheming Duke planned to imprison Mary and put his daughter-in-law, Lady Jane Grey, on the throne to retain the power he had exercised over Edward VI. He had told Mary to go to London to see her ailing brother but had not told her that the King was already dead. The Queen sought temporary sanctuary with her supporters, the Huddlestons of Sawston Hall, who gave her shelter. Early the next morning, disguised as a milkmaid, the Queen continued her flight. It is said that she looked back to see Sawston Hall in flames. Northumberland's soldiers had torched the manor, destroying a large part of the Hall in the process. Mary vowed to repay her hosts and was as good as her word. With her help Sir John and Edmund Huddleston gradually rebuilt Sawston Hall between 1557 and 1584. The accession of Elizabeth I in 1558 meant that a number of priests' holes were secretly incorporated in the refurbishments.

During the Second World War, the United States Army Air Force occupied the Hall as an operations base, though the house remained in the ownership of the Huddleston family. In the early 1960s author Diana Norman visited Sawston Hall together with photographer Jeremy Grayson and clairvoyant Tom Corbett. At that time the Hall's owners were Captain Reginald Eyre-Huddleston and his wife Clare Huddleston, who was the granddaughter of a former Duke of Norfolk. Diana Norman wrote of her meeting with the Huddlestons in her excellent book *The Stately Ghosts of England*. Clare had just married Reginald in 1930 when she came to Sawston and she often heard the sound of a spinet being played. 'The first time,' she said, 'I was standing in the hall at the foot of the stairs, and I heard this music quite distinctly. The only musical instrument we had in the house was the old harpsichord, and I knew it wasn't that. The tone was much lighter. Besides, there was nobody playing the harpsichord.' Sometime after this, one of Clare's friends who was staying with the family asked 'What is that tinkly music I keep hearing?' Clare spoke to a retired maid who served at the great house in the latter part of the nineteenth century. She said that there were always three long knocks on the Tapestry Room door, which would then open and a grey shape would float across the room. She had been kneeling down setting the fire there one morning when it had happened to her. She actually saw this 'grey thing' pass by her. 'She was so frightened she ran out of the room into the Little Gallery and fell down the steps which lead into it, hurting herself badly.'

Clairvoyant Tom Corbett was to spend a sleepless night at Sawston in the Tapestry Bedroom, a large chamber, named after the ceiling to floor Flemish tapestries of Bible scenes that hung there. Its focal point was the Queen Mary bed, an elegant, canopied four-poster in which she spent her disturbed night on 7 July 1553. Corbett knew nothing of the haunted history and insisted that no-one tell him anything as he wanted to form his own impressions, without prejudice. He came downstairs in the morning looking tired out and he had news for Captain and Mrs Huddleston.

I have had a very fatiguing night. Your ghost has woken me every hour on the hour since four o'clock. I have an alarm clock, a very good alarm clock, which I set for seven a.m. when I went to bed last night. It went off at four, although it was still set for seven, and I woke up to hear someone fiddling with the latch of the door. The alarm went off again at five; again the alarm hand was still pointing to seven, and I heard someone prowling around the Panelled Room behind me. The same thing happened at six, and again I had the sense of someone checking my room. Do you know what I think your ghost is? A night watchman, it is definitely a man and it is definitely protective. I should imagine he was employed as a watchman here once, and has now taken the job of looking after the house at night, seeing that no harm comes to it. There's no harm in him. At one point a word which sounded like 'Cutlass' kept flashing into my mind. I think it was the ghost's name. Does it mean anything to you?

The Huddlestons had not heard of such a name but there was an interesting footnote. Sometime after Diana Norman's visit to Sawston, she received a letter from Mrs Huddleston. She wrote, 'Since your visit, in fact only yesterday, we have found out that there is a family in the village called "Cutriss". This is quite extraordinary as we have never heard of it, and it could so easily be the name that Mr Corbett was hearing.'

Tom Corbett's experiences were shared with other overnight guests who stayed in the Tapestry Room. A young undergraduate came to stay and he had a bad cold. As Mrs Huddleston was short of room she put him in Queen Mary's bed in the haunted room. In the morning he thanked his hostess for looking in on him during the night. She assured him that she had done no such thing. He then proceeded to tell her that he had heard someone outside his room in the small hours and then a knocking on his door. There was a fiddling with the latch, but nobody came in. Another witness to the hauntings was a Catholic priest, a Father Martindale, who stayed in another bedroom near the Tapestry Room. He reported having a terribly disturbed night and that periodically there had been someone rapping on his door.

Ghost hunter Peter Underwood did some investigating of his own, following up on the story that he had heard, that Queen Mary's ghost haunted the house and grounds. He spoke with a Mrs Fuller, who was cook to the Huddlestons and she told him that she had seen the ghost herself, 'without the shadow of a doubt'. 'She did not speak but just drifted out of the room. I could never spend a night here by myself, I just couldn't.'

Captain Huddleston's nephew, Major Anthony Eyre, was the next owner of Sawston Hall and one day he was preparing the house for opening to the public. He was alone when he heard the unmistakable sound of girls' laughter floating down from the upper floor. The Major made an immediate search of the house but found nobody. Some years later the ceiling of the Great Hall fell in and Sawston was closed to the public.

By 1982, the cost of running and maintaining Sawston Hall had finally become too much of a financial burden for the Huddleston family and they were forced to sell up. The building was used as an English language school for many years before being sold again in 2004 to internet entrepreneur Adrian Critchlow. In 2008 plans were afoot to transform the Tudor mansion into a luxury hotel and the following year saw extensive renovations carried out to the mansion. Cardinal Cormac Murphy

O'Connor became patron of a campaign to save this most famous of Catholic houses from the developers and instead turn it into a Catholic Heritage Centre. The Priests' Hole and the chapel are of particular architectural importance to Catholics. The Catholic Church continues to monitor the situation and its vigilance will prevent this stunning Tudor Estate from falling into the hands of property developers who may be unsympathetic to its special history. In 2010, Stephen Coates and his family bought Sawston Hall together with its 55 acres of gardens and historic parkland. Recent valuations put the property in the £3 million price bracket so I'll have to wait for that elusive lottery win to enable me to purchase my dream home ...

STEEPLE MORDEN

The former airfield on the road to Littlington has always fascinated me and it came as no surprise to learn that it is haunted. There is not much left of the original base any more, just a few buildings, part of the runway and perimeter track. There is also a memorial with an aircraft propeller as the centrepiece which was dedicated in May 1981 to the brave souls who gave their lives in the Second World War. At Littlington, I enjoyed a pint at the Crown pub, which has its own tribute with memorabilia and photos depicting life on the airfield. The relationship between flyers and villagers was obviously a warm one and the history of the airfield is full of interest.

Construction began in 1939 and the airfield was opened in 1940; initially it was home to an Operations Training Unit equipped with Wellington bombers but the site was to be most closely associated with the Americans. On 12 October 1942 the first US forces arrived in the shape of the 12th Photographic Reconnaissance Squadron and on 25 October the 15th Photographic Mapping Squadron of the 3rd Photographic Group joined them, under the command of Colonel Elliott C. Roosevelt, the American President's son. His squadron's stay was short – they moved on at the end of November. A strange event occurred in February 1942 when a German JU 88 bomber crash landed at Steeple Morden. The pilot, thinking he was over France, had become totally disorientated. The crew was swiftly captured and taken to nearby Bassingbourn for interrogation.

In July 1943, the American 355 Fighter Group appeared at Steeple Morden which was renamed station F-122. Initially, the squadron was equipped with P-47 Thunderbolts and later with P-51 Mustangs. This fighter group received a unit citation for extraordinary heroism and outstanding performance. The group's record for scoring the highest number of enemy aircraft destroyed on the ground earned them the sobriquet 'Steeple Morden Strafers'. They saw action at the D-Day landings and in July 1945 they departed for the last time – bound for Gablingen in Germany, as part of the Army of Occupation. The airfield was closed in September 1946 and the land was returned to its original owners – George Jarman, George Smyth and Bert Parrish.

The site of Steeple Morden Airfield, where ghostly voices have been heard.

At Christmas time in 2001 a telecoms engineer with an interest in the Second World War was passing the old airfield site. He decided to stop for a visit, to see what remained of the one-time USAAF fighter base. It looked decidedly unpromising – hoar frost covered the ground and visibility was down to 50–60 feet in an all-encompassing fog. As is the way in such conditions, all was silent – until the lone visitor distinctly heard the sound of American voices. They were talking quite loudly and occasionally laughing. Although heard clearly, there was no distinguishing what was actually being said. There was nobody about to account for the disembodied voices. Then a car drove past and when the noise from its passing disappeared all was silent once again. The witness later said that he 'felt creepy but not scared', the incident 'gave me a chill'.

WEST WRATTING

Situated on low ground some five miles north of Linton is West Wratting, which has a number of ghost stories surrounding it. In the 1970s this village's Weston Colville Hall was said to be haunted by 'a phantom unique in its peculiarity'. The Hall was built in 1725 as a country mansion for a wealthy gentleman farmer. By the 1970s it was divided into several separate units, two of which were elegant homes and the third was the administrative offices of the D'Abo estates. In 1973, Andrew and Marion Dodkin with their baby daughter moved into part of the mansion. Before they could set up home the place had to be thoroughly redecorated, so a working party of relatives and friends got to work in the evenings. Around

7 p.m. one mid-May evening, Andy Dodkin's mother and father, having taken their turn with the wallpapering upstairs, decided to leave. As they came downstairs Mrs Dodkin saw someone else in the house, an elderly woman, that she didn't recognise, who hurried to the kitchen window, peered out, then turned back to face her. The stranger had greying reddish hair and a high complexion. She was dressed in a sharp-waisted long black dress with a white collar and long sleeves. The woman in the old-fashioned dress frowned and then hurried out of sight the way she had come. Mrs Dodkin rushed into the kitchen and the elderly lady was still there. Mrs Dodkin later reported, 'There were straight lines both sides of the figure as if I were watching her through a gap in a vertically boarded fence (or through another dimension?) a gap that moved about with her as she went to and fro.' This same apparition was seen on at least two subsequent occasions. In 1975, an agricultural student returned late one night to pick up her car from Weston Colville Hall and seeing a light on in the kitchen assumed that Marion Dodkin was there. She went to the house for a cup of coffee and a chat. As she passed a window she saw what she took to be Marion, working at the table. On reaching the kitchen the student found it empty and in darkness, as was the entire house.

Deep snow drifts in the harsh winter of 1976 delayed Andy Dodkin on his way home from work. He arrived home a worried man as he had not been able to find a telephone box to call his wife. Marion, too, had been anxious. As Andy stood outside Weston Colville Hall he wasn't surprised by the sight of Marion standing in the window of the spare room he used as an office. She was staring down the road and she was lit up by the light filtering in from behind her, as the office door was open. Andy hurried indoors only to discover his wife fast asleep in bed; it was obvious that she must have been so for some time. He immediately checked the office and the rest of the house, which was deserted.

The elder Mrs Dodkin made enquiries in the village and several older residents immediately recognised the ghost from the accurate description they were given. It was a fairly recent apparition, either Mrs Savage or her sister Mrs Wilby. The sisters habitually dressed in this fashion and they had lived in the Hall until after the Second World War.

West Wratting is also associated with sightings of a spectral black dog with a difference – it was said to have the face of a monkey! Although this unusual manifestation has not been reported here since the Second World War, another local apparition has been seen in fairly recent times. This is the 'white lady', who walks from Concordia House, a fine, Georgian-style house (which originally dates from the 1500s) on the common to Spanney's Gate, leading into West Wratting Park. She has been described as 'glowing in an unearthly light', but she seems to be a harmless ghost.

Another story from West Wratting comes from the files of Ghost Research Foundation International. Mrs X bought Hill Cottage in West Wratting and soon after moving in her husband (whom she later divorced) took on a different personality. He became a reckless spendthrift and womaniser. The locals compared his behaviour to Dave's (the deceased son of the previous owner of Hill Cottage). All the inhabitants of the cottage, including the dog, were to experience paranormal incidents. One day Mr X thought he saw his wife at the top of the stairs, wearing a long dress, but, on investigation, he found her fast asleep in bed. Every night at 8 p.m. the family dog would regularly sniff at the study door in an agitated manner for about ten minutes before settling again. Mrs X's toddler son was woken by a man 'with a horrible face'. Mrs X was moving a bed downstairs to the study but it got stuck on the staircase and she was about to seek help when it suddenly became much easier to manoeuvre. She was able to guide it into position using just one hand. She was later told that this would have been impossible, as all the furniture that had previously been placed in that room was taken in through the windows. At another time, while she was clearing out an inglenook fireplace, she felt a hand on her back and this invisible hand was felt by her again, on several occasions. Visitors were also affected by the ghosts. On numerous occasions overnight guests who stayed in the spare bedroom reported seeing a figure in the middle of the night. It stood there, staring at them. Mrs X avoided this room as much as possible; it had a strange atmosphere that made her feel most uncomfortable. Probably the strangest incident of all was the disappearing (and reappearing) silver cigarette box. It regularly vanished from the coffee table on a Tuesday and reappeared in the same place on a Thursday. After two years the couple were forced to move out as Mr X hadn't paid the mortgage for six months. His ex-wife said, 'I never did find out about the history of that haunted cottage, but I was glad to leave.'

SHINGAY-CUM-WENDY

During the early 1990s, Thatched Cottage Audio was the biggest Pro Audio Retailer in the country. It had music studios in some old outbuildings called Minstrel Court based at Shingay-cum-Wendy near Arrington. Phil Darke worked here in his younger days when in his late twenties and early thirties. One night at about 11 p.m., Phil answered the door to his Royston home and standing on the threshold were two of his colleagues, Pete and Mark. They were clearly in a state of shock and pleaded with Phil to accompany them back to Minstrel Court. The pair were too scared to return unaccompanied so Phil obliged. Pete had a small private studio at the opposite end of the buildings from the main Minstrel studios. While he was in his studio the mains power had tripped out (quite a common occurrence attributed to the mains system being inadequate). Pete and Mark went up to the trip switch which was located in the pool room, just outside Phil's room. They heard strange noises coming from the locked and empty studio that freaked them out. The pair later described it as sounding like metal bolts being slid shut. Pete and Mark fled, terrified. Phil, Pete and Mark returned that night; Phil turned the mains back on and unlocked his studio, which was, as it should have been, unoccupied.

After Thatched Cottage Audio went into receivership Phil Darke carried on renting the studio premises. When he was installing the studio his wife Gaynor heard the sound of someone playing a keyboard, but it was coming from an empty studio. One Sunday at lunchtime Phil was working alone with the door to his studio open when he heard someone open the external door and come into the pool room next to his studio. Looking up he saw a figure reflected in the matt white paint of his studio door. Curious, he got up to see who his visitor was, but there was nobody there.

In 2010, Phil Darke revisited the old Thatched Cottage premises on business and asked owner David Simpson if strange things still happened but initially he seemed to be quite dismissive. The businessman retained the premises after Thatched Cottage Audio went out of business. He still lives in the house and now runs a new enterprise there. David did admit to one unexplained occurrence: at night his television, situated downstairs, would come on at full volume waking him and his family up. He had thought that this was down to his young son until brother-in-law Phil Mould was house sitting alone one night when the same thing happened. It was to be a most eventful time. Earlier Phil Darke saw some equipment meters moving around (but not by any human agency) in the studio. He also received phone calls from unoccupied areas of the building. The internal phone system allowed one phone to buzz another phone elsewhere in the building. When the phone buzzed it was possible to identify which phone was calling by which light was flashing on the instrument.

That same evening Phil Mould was helping Phil Darke to lock and alarm the whole premises when the internal phone next to them buzzed. The light on the top of the phone indicated that the call was coming from the downstairs extension in the house. Across the courtyard the pair of them could clearly see the actual phone on the sideboard, it was unattended.

WARESLEY

In his book *Mysterious Cambridgeshire*, author Daniel Codd mentions a case from the files of the highly respected Society for Psychical Research concerning Waresley village. The village is situated close to Gamlingay, near the border with Bedfordshire, and in 1966 a Mrs Herbert moved here from Australia to take up residence at Vicarage Farm. On her first night in her new home, Mrs Herbert was trying to get to sleep when she saw the apparition of a small boy kneeling by her bed. She reported that the figure had a 'thin, drawn face' and seemed to be in great distress. Mrs Herbert could feel the little lad's small fingers on her arm and her instincts told her that he was missing his mother. The frightened woman managed to blurt out one word, 'Mummy', and with that the vision dematerialised. Mysterious indeed …

CHAPTER EIGHT

Paranormal Peterborough

BURGHLEY HOUSE

Peterborough extends from Burghley, in the north of Cambridgeshire, to Stilton, in the south. Many people erroneously believe that Burghley House is in Lincolnshire but it is not. The county border between Lincolnshire and Cambridgeshire actually passes between the town and the house. Burghley House is best known for its famous annual Horse Trials yet it is less well known for its hauntings. This magnificent Elizabethan mansion was built by William Cecil, Lord High Treasurer to Queen Elizabeth I, between 1555 and 1577. The north wing, however, wasn't completed until 1587. The building was modelled on the privy lodgings of Richmond Palace. In the eighteenth century, the surrounding parkland was laid out by Capability Brown for the 9th Earl of Exeter. (William Cecil was created 1st Baron Burghley and his descendants were the Earls and Marquesses of Exeter.) Lady Victoria Latham was a daughter of the 6th Marquess of Exeter.

I am indebted to Victoria Latham's book *Burghley: The Life of a Great House* for the following example of a haunting. This is quoted from a former guide who worked at this wonderful stately home. 'I was walking across the rooms closing up for the night, it was about ten minutes to six. I opened the door into the Fourth George (room) and a very cross male voice said, just by my shoulder, "Oh a pax on it." Obviously a spectral inhabitant who thought he was free of pesky visitors for the day. Secondly, I had the impression one day of a tall male figure dressed in black beside the fireplace; a blink and it was gone, but the feeling remained that he was there.'

A TALE OF TWO CATHEDRALS

Cambridgeshire is graced with not one but two Cathedrals, one of which is Ely in the Fenlands. The Anglo-Saxons founded a number of monasteries in the far north of Cambridgeshire and the Abbey of St Peter was one of them. The Abbey church became the Cathedral in 1539, after Henry VIII dissolved the monastery. The Abbey had been run by the Benedictine Order of monks, known as the Blackfriars,

Burghley House is haunted by the apparition of an unknown man.

Peterborough Cathedral: invisible choirs, hooded apparitions and a phantom candle flame have been detected in the building.

since their robes were black and their work ethics strict. The monastery and the town that grew up around it already had a history of violence. The Vikings invaded during the late sixth century and attacked and destroyed Peterborough. Some 400 years later the town was subjected to further destruction. Hereward the Wake, during his war of English resistance against his hated Norman conquerors, led an army of Viking mercenaries in a raid on Peterborough in 1069.

Henry VIII's first wife, Queen Catherine of Aragon, was buried at Peterborough in 1536. Their daughter, Mary, was temporarily laid to rest here too, following her execution at Fotheringhay Castle in 1587. Mary Queen of Scots body was later (in 1612) moved to London's Westminster Abbey, where it still lies.

The Cathedral, like its counterpart at Ely, is famously haunted by a variety of phenomena. It seems that the former monks who inhabited the old abbey are as reluctant to leave their former home as the phantom monks of Ely. The best sighting is probably the monk seen walking in the ruined cloisters at the side of Peterborough Cathedral. He has often been mistaken for a real person but for the fact that he manifests from a doorway blocked up with stonework and dematerialises into a locked door at the side of the Cathedral. This hooded figure is regularly reported, usually several times a year. Another monk, said to be mischievous, is familiarly known as 'Benedict' by the staff in the Tourist Information Centre.

An unseen choir is sometimes heard in the building, singing in Latin, when there is no sign of any human presence. One well-documented incident is the historian's story from 1958. Trevor Bevis, while visiting the Cathedral one November day, clearly heard Vespers sung in Latin, but there was no sign of any living occupants in the choir stalls that day. Then he sensed the monks' presence all around, as though they were singing for him. After several minutes the singing ceased and as the listener made his way out of the building he encountered the verger in the nave. Trevor told him about his extraordinary experience and the verger confirmed that a few other people had told him of similar auditory phenomena that they had heard. Although Trevor was a regular visitor to the Cathedral he never experienced the ghostly chorus again.

A candle is occasionally glimpsed, burning in a West Front window of the Cathedral. It is reputed to be the light of a long dead stonemason, one of the original builders. He was working late one night when he lost his footing in the darkness and tumbled to his death from the high scaffolding.

Another apparition that has been clearly described by witnesses is that of a very young monk, aged about twenty, wearing a black habit. Observers say that he looks tired and hungry as he walks up the Cathedral Nave before stopping and looking behind him. On turning back he appears panic stricken, then sets off in a terrified run before vanishing near the front of the Nave. It has been speculated that this may be a re-enactment of a monk in flight from Viking raiders and he vanishes because he was caught and slaughtered at this point.

There is also a well-known haunted house in the precincts of the Cathedral. The ghost of a young girl has been seen at a first-floor window. The story is that she was murdered in this room sometime in the 1860s, by her own father.

A HAUNTED RAILWAY STATION

The Nene Valley Railway extends seven and a half miles between the Peterborough Nene Valley and Yarwell Junction. Wansford railway station is the main station for the Nene Valley Railway. Sited between Stibbington and Water Newton Wansford is reputedly a most haunted location. Ghost hunters and thrill seekers from all over the country regularly converge at the station to spend the night on vigils in hopes of experiencing unexplained phenomena. The reason for this enthusiasm is that there have been at least half a dozen sightings of ghostly figures seen on the platform and in the toilet area. There are even reports of phantoms caught on CCTV and doors have been seen to swing open to admit unseen visitors.

PETERBOROUGH'S HAUNTED AIRFIELD

RAF Wittering, situated just to the north of Peterborough, is one of a mere handful of survivors out of the twenty military airfields that once covered the county of Cambridgeshire during the Second World War. This particular military airfield has seen many changes of use and is one of the oldest in the country. It dates back to 1916 when the Royal Air Force was formed out of what had previously been the Royal Flying Corps. Back then its biplane fighters' role was as anti-Zeppelin interceptors. RAF Wittering later became home to flying training, prior to the arrival of number 38 Squadron, equipped with Hurricanes (in 1938) when the base returned to fighter station status. Hurricanes from the station were heavily involved in the Battle of Britain. The airfield's distinguished war record included the destruction of 151 enemy aircraft and 89 flying bombs with a further 112 Luftwaffe machines damaged or possibly destroyed by the station's Spitfires and Hurricanes. The airfield was bombed on no less than five occasions; the heaviest raid in March 1941 saw one officer and sixteen airmen killed.

In 1948, RAF Wittering returned to Flying Training Command and became home to Number 1 Initial Training School. During 1952–54, a 9,050-foot-long concrete runway was built to enable the unit to re-role as a Bomber Command station and ushered in the Jet Age. RAF Wittering was equipped with the four-jet Vickers Valiant bomber, part of the new strategic Nuclear Deterrent Force, known as the V-force, throughout the 1950s and 1960s. Atomic bomb tests were carried out in Central Australia during Operation Buffalo in 1956. From 1956 to 1958, nine hydrogen bombs were dropped over Malden Island and Christmas Island during Operation Grapple. By 1968, the V bomber force was redundant and the station changed yet again to become 'the Home of the Harrier'. Number 1 Fighter Squadron arrived in August 1969 – the first unit in the world to operate vertical or short take-off and landing (VSTOL) aircraft. The squadron served with distinction in the Falklands campaign and later in the Balkans, Serbia and Kosovo, until its departure in August 2000 to RAF Cottesmore.

In 2006, the primary role of RAF Wittering altered yet again when it became home to the Headquarters of the RAF's Expeditionary Logistics Force (A4 Force). In 2011, Number 85 Expeditionary Logistics Wing based at Wittering played a crucial role in the enforcement of the no-fly zone in Libya. Convoys of up to twenty-one articulated lorries regularly shuttled between Wittering and Italy, involving round trips of some 3,500 miles. They delivered over 3,500 tons of spare parts, generators and other equipment – front-line supplies for the air forces' Typhoon and Tornado fighters. RAF Wittering's future looks assured; as well as continuing as an RAF base it will, from 2015, also house army personnel returning from Germany.

As is the case at a number of other haunted airfields, the phenomena at the station seem to centre on the old control tower. A ghostly bomber reputedly haunts the airfield; it has been reported as silently descending until reaching ground level then disappearing. At other times it has been seen to crash into the control tower. This is said to be a recording type haunting, a recreation of an incident that happened early in the Second World War when a bomber that was in difficulties attempted an emergency landing at the fighter base, but crashed into the control tower – many airmen were killed in the disaster. Phantom airmen have been seen around the crash site. The control tower also appears to be haunted by an unseen 'presence' and lights are switched on by invisible fingers while unexplained loud bangs are heard in the building. Footsteps are heard in the empty corridor of what used to be the old hanger for Number 1 Squadron at RAF Wittering and moving shadows have been seen in the rooms here.

WOODCROFT CASTLE

One well-known and gruesome ghost associated with Peterborough is that which inhabits Woodcroft Castle, situated five miles to the north-west of the town. Built in the thirteenth century as a fortified manor house, Woodcroft Castle is extremely hard to find. It is a turreted old fortress with battlements, round towers, a moat and mysterious dark windows. It is not open to the public as it is privately owned.

During the English Civil Wars, Woodcroft Castle was the home of ardent Royalist Dr Michael Hudson, who was Charles I's guardian. In 1645, at the Battle of Naseby, the Royalist army was crushed by the forces commanded by Fairfax and Cromwell and the war was effectively lost for King Charles I. Minor battles, skirmishes and mopping up operations continued however. In 1648, Dr Michael Hudson was besieged at his home by Parliamentarian soldiers under Colonel Woodhead. Woodhead's brother-in-law led the first, unsuccessful attack and was killed. The enraged colonel personally led the second attack and succeeded in breaching the defences. Hudson was chased to the battlements where he attempted to hide by climbing over and clinging to the top with his fingertips. A Roundhead discovered him, however, and slashed the unfortunate man's hands off at the wrists so that he fell into the moat. He was then dragged from the water, still alive, and his tongue was ripped out by vengeful soldiers. This was one of many atrocities committed by the Parliamentarian Army, to their eternal shame. Not surprisingly Dr Hudson died soon after this final mutilation. His ghost continues to haunt his old home, the scene of his grisly death.

After the capture of Woodcroft Castle, Dr Hudson's tongue was sent around the country as a grim trophy, while screams were heard at night, echoing from the battlements of his former home. Anguished cries of 'Mercy, mercy' and sounds of swordplay continued to be heard by terrified witnesses. Two of the Roundhead soldiers involved in the savagery ended their days badly. One suffered a horrific death when his gun exploded, while the other, who travelled around the country for a time exhibiting Hudson's tongue, fell on hard times and died in abject poverty.

It is said that Dr Hudson's dreadful end is annually re-enacted in ethereal form, when ghostly screams are heard. It is also said that his is not the only phantom in this haunted hideaway.

MANIFESTATIONS AT THE MUSEUM

In answer to my question about the most haunted place in Cambridgeshire, my friend Martin Waldock's reply was unequivocal, 'Peterborough Museum'. I have known Martin for many years as we share a common interest as researchers into the paranormal. He is one of the founders of the CPRS, Cambridge Paranormal Research Society, so he knows the county intimately. The story he related about the museum was intriguing, but more of that later.

The building which is Peterborough Museum dates from the time of King George III, 1816, and it was the townhouse of Thomas and Charlotte Cooke until 1856, when Queen Victoria was on the throne. It was then sold to the 3rd Earl Fitzwilliam who gave his permission for it to be used as the city's first hospital in 1856, when it was established as the Public Infirmary and Fever Hospital and so it continued until 1928. The present Conservation Room is the original Operating Theatre. In the late 1800s, Peterborough Natural History Society & Field Club began collecting items for the museum; these exhibits can be seen today. The collection of artefacts has grown to over 200,000 items. This impressive Georgian building, situated on Priestgate, became the Museum in 1931 but then its layout was very different to today's layout. The Art Gallery had not been built on the back, the top floor was rented out as office space and the only full-time staff were the caretaker and his wife, who lived here with their two children. The Yarrow family's flat on the first floor today forms part of the Geology Gallery. It soon became evident to the Yarrows that the building was haunted. In 1932, Mrs Yarrow and her daughter were alarmed to hear footsteps in the empty Norman Cross Room (formerly the Women's Surgical Ward) between 8 and 9.30 p.m.

On a September day in 1931, Mr Yarrow went out with his sons for the afternoon, leaving his wife at home alone. She dealt with the last few visitors to the museum and locked up for the day. Returning to the flat, Mrs Yarrow started preparing the evening meal ready for her family's return. After about half an hour she heard a noise on the main staircase and assumed it was her loved ones returning so she went out to greet them. Instead she was confronted by a stranger coming upstairs. She described him later as a young man aged about thirty, with brown hair and wearing a green or grey coloured suit. Assuming, at first, that this was a visitor she had locked in by mistake she quickly realised that something was amiss. The stranger's footsteps seemed unnaturally loud – yet he was in fact floating up the stairs. He reached the landing in front of her and drifted through the closed doors beside the startled caretaker's wife. She saw him passing down the corridor before dematerialising at the far end, at which point she made a hasty exit from the building.

The apparition seen by Mrs Yarrow is believed to be that of a soldier, Thomas Hunter, who died in the building some fifteen years previously. At that time the place was being used as a temporary hospital. Thomas Hunter was born in Newcastle in 1880, but as a young man he emigrated to Australia where, in New South Wales, he found work as a coalminer. At the outbreak of the First World War he enlisted with the Australian Army, the ANZACS, where he became a sergeant and served in both Gallipoli, Turkey, and on the Western Front. In June 1916, he was seriously wounded and he was treated in a field hospital before being shipped back to Britain for treatment in a more specialised hospital. Sergeant Hunter was put on a train heading north but his condition worsened so the train was halted at a convenient station – Peterborough. The Australian soldier was taken to the nearest hospital (what is now the museum), but it was too late for him. He died in hospital on 31 July 1916 and was buried in Peterborough's Broadway Cemetery. The ghost of the lonely ANZAC sergeant, who died so far from home, has been seen on a number of occasions; the last time was in the 1970s.

A sudden, unexpected cold atmosphere has been detected in certain parts of the museum in recent times. Some people have reported the touch of ice-cold hands and furniture is regularly found mysteriously moved around overnight. It has been estimated that there are at least ten different ghosts, which adds weight to any consideration that this is Cambridgeshire's most haunted location.

Manifestations occur on a weekly basis, further reinforcing the claim. The cellar is one paranormal 'hot spot' (or should that be cold spot?) with a variety of manifestations reported. These include 'a sinister presence', unexplained noises, objects unaccountably moved, phantom breath felt and the figure of a monk seen as well as the apparition of a small animal reported to be either a white cat or dog. Other parts of the museum have been known to exhibit a variety of phenomena such as mysterious lights, poltergeist-like effects and Roman soldiers have been glimpsed. Peterborough Museum now regularly hosts 'fright nights' when visitors (for a fee) can spend an evening in the company of its many mysterious entities. The ultimate ghost hunting accolade was bestowed in April 2005, when the team from television's *Most Haunted* spent an eventful night here, assuring Peterborough Museum's ghostly fame for many years to come. The team from the popular programme fled when the cellar door inexplicably slammed on them.

CPRS INVESTIGATES

On a summer's night in August 2003, a team from Cambridge Paranormal Research Society undertook a vigil at Peterborough Museum. A team of nine investigators divided into three teams: Martin, Rob and Julie were in Group A, Dave, Elaine and Giles were in Group B, and Paul, Angela and Stuart were in Group C. The plan was to establish, for one hour's duration, observation points, situated on the ground, first and second floors. The CPRS members initially walked through the building to orientate themselves. Then they began their baseline readings at 10.22 p.m. These readings were to measure air pressure, humidity, temperature and electromagnetic frequencies at the start of the vigil. Comparisons with these initial baselines were taken throughout the night, to see what changes, if any, occurred. Carefully chosen trigger objects were distributed around the premises. A 1936 penny was left in the Lecture Room. An 1899 penny and a cross were placed in the sentry box (Social History Area). A ring and a halfpenny were put in the kitchen (Social History Area). Closed circuit television infrared cameras were set up in the Meeting Room with a recording station in the office. Infrared cameras plus motion sensors were placed on the first floor stair landing. The Restoration Room was locked off as was the first floor corridor, which had a recording station located there.

The CPRS team were in for an interesting night. In the Temporary Exhibition Area Dave received a mental image of a young, long-haired girl dancing around the room and laughing. He kept this impression to himself and asked Giles if he picked up anything. Without any hesitation Giles replied that he could see a young girl ... and she was laughing. Dave was later watching the monitor in the Office when he heard a noise from the next door Lecture Room. No-one was in this room

The CPRS crew at the Peterborough Museum investigation.

at the time. As he continued to watch the monitor he noticed a spherical light flashing slowly on, and then gradually moving off across the screen. He checked the Lecture Room but could find nothing that might have caused either the sound or the light.

At 1 a.m. the trigger objects in the Geology Section had moved significantly. Soon after 3 a.m. the team gathered downstairs for a full discussion and report on the night's events. At 4 a.m. it was decided to hold one last vigil, with the complete group, in the Geology Department on the first floor. As they settled themselves on the floor Martin and Paul thought that someone else was on the landing, about to come in. They were puzzled when no-one did and made a quick head count to see who was missing. No-one was missing and at that point Dave mentioned that when everyone had been ascending the stairs towards the corridor he had been at the front. He had the distinct impression that someone else had been just ahead of him and that someone had already gone into the Geology Area. He thought that he caught a glimpse of a person going through the door ahead of the team. All the investigators were as sure as they could be that no-one else had been in the museum at this time. The CPRS team were a little disappointed not to have captured any hard evidence on their stills cameras, video cameras or digital sound recorders. There was also a lack of significant change on the data recorders, nothing that was noteworthy. Every team member, however, shared the feeling that the group had not been alone in the building that night. The most active areas were on the first floor stairs and corridor landing as well as the Lecture Room and the end of the corridor close by the area associated with the servants' stairs. The CPRS report concluded with the proposition that, with Peterborough Museum 'housing so many social and ancient artefacts and given its occupation as a house and a hospital there were a plethora of connections to possible spirit activity there. A great deal of further research would be necessary to uncover the many hidden truths buried beneath its ethereal fabric.'

MEETING AT THE MUSEUM

I decided to do some more research into Peterborough's most famously haunted location. I met the man who knows more than anyone about the museum as well as all the other many haunted sites in and around Peterborough. Stuart Orme is the Marketing and Events Manager/Historian at Peterborough Museum. He is the man who organises the night vigils for both members of the public and paranormal investigation groups. He is also the man who spends sleepless nights working as a guide for the multitude of ghost hunters who want to experience this haunted venue at first hand. He leads the ghost walks around the town, which start from the museum. Stuart confirmed my belief that this site is one of the most interesting places in the whole of the UK for anyone with a serious interest in unexplained phenomena. We had a long and informative talk so that now I can reveal the facts about this special place. Here are some of the paranormal 'hotspots':

Norman Room – Second Floor

Disembodied voices – both male and female – have been heard in this room which has a carpeted floor. This doesn't stop the sounds of phantom footsteps, described as sounding 'like leather shoes on a wooden floor'. (Underneath the carpet there are teak floors.)

Victorian Room – Second Floor

Groaning noises have been heard from this room.

Back Staircase – Second Floor

Psychic mediums have picked up on a lady being pushed down the stairs by a male. Mediums (particularly women) have also felt hands on their back. Legend has it that when this was a private home a servant girl was raped by one of the 'gentlemen' of the house. The unfortunate girl fell pregnant and was allegedly pushed downstairs 'as a solution to the problem'. It is believed that she fell to her death.

Roman Room – First Floor

The spirit of a Roman soldier has been seen – it is thought that he is connected with a sword that is on display here. At times this room is extremely active. Monks' chanting has been heard during day time (there are mannequins of monks on display).

Prehistoric Room – First Floor

This is another room where disembodied voices have been heard.

Shop Area – First Floor

One particular corner is very psychically active – noises are regularly heard and people have been touched by unseen hands. A lady who likes to push and shove visitors is said to be responsible for the bangs that are sometimes heard in this room.

Landing (Between Ground and First Floor)

A 'lady of status' has been seen here – there is an item on display which is said to be connected to her.

Cellar

A 'partial' manifestation (of a hand/arm) has been seen, a fairly rare occurrence in the history of paranormal sightings. In February 2009, the hooded figure of a monk/priest was seen by a number of witnesses. In April 2009, items were thrown at ghost hunters stationed in the cellar. In the most haunted property in the most haunted city this is undoubtedly the scariest and most haunted room of all.

There would seem to be at least seven apparitions which haunt Peterborough Museum:

1. Grey figure, thought to be 'the lonely ANZAC', Thomas Hunter, who was born in Newcastle and who died here from wounds received in France on 31 July 1916 (seen on the stairs and the first floor corridor). A medium has suggested that Thomas returns in visitation, walking around the building.

2. Kitchen maid who fell to her death on the back stairs.

3. Dark, male presence, seen and felt lurking near the re-created period shop on the first floor.

4. Roman soldier – said to be connected with his sword for all eternity, seen by a visitor as recently as September 2006.

5. White lady, who follows visitors around the upper floor, seen by two visitors in October 2008.

6. Little girl, rarely seen, in the Geology Gallery. She leaves EVP (electronic voice phenomena) messages on audio recordings and she terrified a workman who saw her in December 2008.

7. Monk-like figure seen in the cellar (a particularly eerie place with slamming doors, weird noises and a 'threatening' male presence).

We have the complete range of anomalous phenomena recorded at Peterborough Museum at one time or another. In addition to the previously mentioned manifestations poltergeist activity was reported in a ground floor room where furniture has been found moved overnight. Trigger objects set up in controlled experiments by CPRS were moved. Unaccountable smells have been detected as well as CPRS's sightings of light anomalies. The last words belong to Stuart Orme, who strikes me as one of the most level-headed witnesses I have ever interviewed. He told me, in no uncertain terms, that he has seen the monk that haunts the cellar with his own eyes, on only one occasion, but fortunately the historian was with company at the time ... Peterborough Museum remains unique and unchallenged – it is the most haunted site in the whole of Cambridgeshire.

Author Information

Damien O'Dell's third book in the *Paranormal* series follows on from the success of his earlier works, *Paranormal Bedfordshire* and *Paranormal Hertfordshire*. This time he investigates a place where he once earned his living and in an area that he fell in love with, Cambridgeshire. He is a particular fan of the Fens, a mysterious, remote, and timeless land, with its big skies and endless horizons.

Cambridge town also exerts a strong pull; the author is a frequent visitor here and has enjoyed piecing together the intricate jigsaw of the haunted history of this county town. He continues his odyssey, exploring the paranormal in its many manifestations. Along the way he has formulated his own hypotheses about the unexplained, which he enthusiastically shares with his readers.

In 2007 Damien was approached by the Arthur Findlay College at Stansted Hall to conduct a new residential course – Investigating the Paranormal. He taught students from all over the world how to conduct successful investigations at haunted places, using the knowledge he gained from leading vigils at a multitude of sites across the British Isles.

Damien saw his first ghost at the age of twelve, in West London, in the company of his best friend, Renato. The boys saw an apparition gliding through the gardens of the Grange, a ruined house that had once belonged to a famous artist. The pair believed that they saw the ghost of Sir Edward Coley Burne-Jones, a successful Victorian painter and designer, who died in 1898. After seeing this apparition a lifelong interest in the paranormal was kindled …

BROADCASTS, LECTURES & TRAINING

As well as being a published author, Damien is a broadcaster, lecturer and trainer. He regularly makes broadcasts on both BBC Radio 3 Counties and Chiltern Radio. He has given talks to large audiences at the Ghost Club, the Arthur Findlay College and Belgrave Hall. He has also been guest speaker at history societies, libraries, Rotary Clubs, the Women's Institute and many other groups. He has delivered training to students from all over the world at the annual one-week residential course, 'Investigating the Paranormal'. This is held at the internationally renowned

Arthur Findlay College in Stansted, Essex. Damien is frequently asked to give talks on various paranormal subjects to groups around the country. If you want to contact him his email address is damienodell@yahoo.co.uk and you can visit his new website at www.damienodell.com. His investigation group APIS (Anglia Paranormal Investigation Society) is based in North Hertfordshire and has a number of members from Cambridgeshire. Every member is trained by Damien in the science of Paranormal Investigation, from safety to interviewing techniques. If you want to know more about APIS then visit the society's website www.apisteamspirit.co.uk and if you have any questions the following are examples taken from Damien's talks.

Frequently Asked Questions

What is a ghost?
I don't pretend to know the answer to that and neither does anyone else! However, if we are looking for a definition then this is the generally accepted one – a ghost is a human, witnessed by someone, which cannot be physically present. This is because they are dead (well usually). Sometimes, however, ghosts of the living are reported, when the living person is far removed from the location where their ghost is seen.

What is the difference between a ghost and a poltergeist?
There are numerous differences; whereas ghosts tend to be 'shy' and are often seen by a single witness, poltergeists seem to like company and can 'play to the audience'. Poltergeists can interact with witnesses and may produce phenomena to order. Ghosts are often seemingly unaware of their surroundings and don't interact with their audience. Ghosts are frequently reported to 'glide' rather than to make noisy progress, whereas poltergeists are quite the opposite; indeed their name is German in origin and means 'noisy ghost'. They live up to their nomenclature by producing raps, loud bangs, door slamming and causing objects to move and sometimes to break. They grab our attention by throwing things, producing pools of water and creating small fires or showers of stones. Fortunately the poltergeist's timespan is mercifully short – their 'infestation' often lasts for a matter of months but ghosts can continue to haunt a site for centuries ... Ghosts are associated with buildings or places whereas poltergeists are people-related. There will often be a young person, usually reaching puberty, who is the centre or focus for the poltergeist activity. When this 'focus' leaves the scene the poltergeist activity often follows them.

Can animals detect ghosts?
Yes they can. All dogs, for instance, appear to have a sixth sense – they can see and hear things that are beyond the normal range of human beings. If you walk your dog in an unfamiliar place and it reacts as though facing an enemy (e.g. snarling, barking, hackles raised, refusing to move on) then it is likely that it has encountered something that you cannot see. Better to turn around and go a different route. Those who deliberately use a dog as a 'psychic barometer' in a known haunted

place are conducting a cruel practise. Dogs can become extremely frightened in haunted locations. Cats, however, are more like people in so far as some seem to be psychic whilst others appear to be oblivious to psychic phenomena. Horses appear to react at haunted sites too – they literally can get badly 'spooked'.

Why do ghosts return to haunt a place?
This is probably the most interesting (and most difficult to explain) question that I am asked on a regular basis. Just as I can't say exactly what a ghost is I also can't say with any degree of certainty why ghosts return to haunt a place. I'll have a stab anyway ... It seems to be something to do with the release of strong emotions. People often assume that a suicide or a murder victim is likely to return as a ghost to the site of their demise and they would be correct. The great trauma suffered by someone who takes their own life or who is murdered does account for a large amount of subsequent haunted locations. There are also those benign haunted houses where the reason for the haunting is entirely the opposite – the owners of these properties loved their homes and were extremely happy there. A good example would be Shaw's Corner, which I wrote about in Paranormal Hertfordshire. George Bernard Shaw and his wife spent a happy lifetime in their beloved home in Ayot St Lawrence. So much did they love the place that they had their ashes scattered in the garden. Small wonder then that their housekeeper, Mrs Laden, swore that GBS returned on two occasions and spoke to this startled witness. It is as though powerful emotions somehow tie the ghost to a particular spot...

If a ghost is in the presence of a group of people will everyone see the ghost?
I would be highly suspicious if everybody reported exactly the same sighting at the same time. In cases where a ghost has been witnessed by a number of people simultaneously, observations always seem to differ quite markedly. For example from a group of travellers who encountered the apparitions of long dead Roman soldiers, some saw the soldiers, some just heard sounds of marching and others both saw and heard nothing at all.

Are there ghosts of things as well as people?
Most definitely – in times past, ghostly coaches and sailing ships were seen. In more modern times phantom aircraft, trains, ships and motor cars have all been reported by reliable witnesses.

What is the difference between a ghost and an apparition?
Strictly speaking, a ghost is someone that you knew when they were alive who returns to haunt you after their death. Typically this is a loved one, usually a near relative, but sometimes it may be a close friend who comes back to visit you. An apparition, on the other hand, is a complete stranger – the unknown phantom monk, Roman soldier or cavalier for instance, that is unexpectedly encountered.

What is the most common manifestation?

Full apparitions, i.e. visions that seem to be completely human, solid and life-like, are extremely rare. Probably the most common phenomena reported are audible, and of these, footsteps, in an otherwise empty house, are most likely to be heard.

How else do ghosts make their presence felt?

You may find yourself experiencing the sensation of being touched by an unseen hand. Unexplained smells may be noticed – pipe tobacco, lavender or rose perfume for instance. ALPs (anomalous light phenomena) may be seen, sometimes described as 'fuzzy dots of light'. You may hear raps (or footsteps as mentioned above).

Who is most likely to see a ghost?

Children up to the age of ten are far more likely to see a ghost than all other age groups combined.

When am I most likely to see a ghost?

Neither at midnight nor in the small hours of the morning, as popularly believed, but in the afternoon – around three quarters of all reported cases of haunting occur at that time of day.

Is it only old buildings that are haunted?

Modern buildings can be haunted too – it often depends on the history of the actual site of the house. Past events from a bygone age can affect the present, like the modern apartments built on the site of a former lunatic asylum, which I wrote about in Paranormal Bedfordshire.

ARE YOU UP FOR THE CHALLENGE OF GHOST HUNTING?

If you would like the opportunity to take part in professionally organised ghost watches in Cambridgeshire you can become a member of Anglia Paranormal Investigation Society (APIS). We want to meet like-minded individuals who share our enthusiasm for investigating anomalous phenomena in a scientific manner. APIS works closely with a national group – the Association for the Scientific Study of Anomalous Phenomena (ASSAP) and many of our members are members of both organisations. Damien O'Dell, who founded APIS in 2002, is an Approved Investigator (A.I.) with ASSAP. Whilst the average paranormal investigation group has a life-span of six months to a year, APIS proudly looks forward to celebrating its tenth birthday in 2012! Our Patron is the legendary Peter Underwood (aka 'King of the Ghost Hunters'). Alan Murdie, former Chairman of the Ghost Club, and Michael Lewis, former National Investigations Co-ordinator with ASSAP, are two of our most distinguished members. For more details about us visit our website:

www.apisteamspirit.co.uk

You may also email our Secretary, Vicki O'Dell:

apismail@virgin.net

Having read *Paranormal Cambridgeshire* you may want to share a true life paranormal experience with the author – please feel free to contact him via the APIS email address, as above. APIS is pleased to hear from people who may need assistance in dealing with unexplained phenomena that are affecting their home or place of work. We are all volunteers and do not charge for our help. Similarly, for those of you who have unexplained psychic abilities, we are pleased to offer help and advice on how to deal with those abilities.

APIS has investigated hundreds of cases in the UK and we anticipate investigating many more in the future. We have a vast amount of experience between us and we are glad to share our expertise with other groups. In the past we have conducted joint investigations with Cambridge Paranormal Research Society, Spiral Paranormal, Renegade Paranormal and others. If you are considering setting up a group in your locality we may be able to offer you our help, support and advice.

Happy hunting!

Glossary of Terms

APPARITION
A Stage 4 manifestation that is sometimes but not always visible to the human eye.

BLACK LINES or STREAMS
An energy (or ley) line of negative influence. Black streams absorb and exude negative feelings and vibrations. They can induce illness, headaches and more seriously depression and degenerative diseases. Black streams can be terminated by an experienced dowser who will 'peg' the stream either at the location or remotely. Crystals may also be effective in reversing the stream. Some psychics and mediums have been known to deal effectively with these energies. Black lines attract negative entities and are often linked to the presence and creation of elemental ghosts.

CASPER EFFECT
Another name for Stage 1 ghosts caught on film or video, so named after the fictional 'Casper the friendly ghost', they appear wispy, translucent or transparent.

CLAIRAUDIENT
A medium or psychic who receives information from the other side in the form of sounds.

CLAIRSENTIENT
A medium who receives information from the other side by experiencing feelings, including physical ones.

CLAIRVOYANT
A medium who receives information from the other side by 'feeling' information and relays it in their own words.

DEMATERIALISATION
The dissipation of a materialisation, i.e. when a ghost vanishes or disappears.

ECTOPLASM
A sub-physical substance that can sometimes be seen with the naked eye. The word originates from the Greek ektos and plasma meaning 'exteriorised substance'. The structure of a ghost is believed to be made up of ectoplasm and it apparently takes form in our physical world by manipulating energies such as electricity and human energy. The more energy available, the more physically 'real' the ghost becomes, until it climaxes in a complete manifestation.

ELECTRONIC VOICE PHENOMENA (EVP)
A recording of voices of the dead, which occurs at a frequency not audible to the human ear.

ELEMENTAL GHOST
A non-human ghost form that exists on a lower level of existence than other ghost types. Elemental ghosts are an embodiment of the actions and intents that have taken place in the ghost's haunting ground. They have limited intelligence and are thought to be created by extreme positive or negative energy that is put into a location over a long period of time.

Elemental ghosts can be created by occult ritual; extremes of intent (good or evil) by humans in the location; actions, experiences and emotions that take place at the location, such as murder, torment, suffering, happiness, love, hate, etc.

Elemental ghosts of a positive orientation are often thought of as protectors or sentinels of buildings or locations. The presence of a positive elemental ghost can be beneficial to a place or a person. Elementals of a negative orientation can cause negative effects in much the same way as black streams can.

ESP
Extra Sensory Perception is a power beyond the normal five senses.

ETHER
The fifth element thought to permeate all space. Ether is believed to be the only element conducive to ectoplasm formation.

The acceptance of the existence of ether could help explain why some psychic manifestations appear 'out of thin air' or in apparent levitation and not resting or standing on anything solid. These ghost manifestations are manipulating the ether as a source of stability.

EXORCISM
The ritual of dispersing a ghost from a location or person, usually against its will. Appointed exorcists of various faiths, particularly Roman Catholic, normally conduct these rituals. It is a fact that, even today, every diocese in Britain has its

own appointed exorcist, aithough the Church keeps this area of its work closely guarded.

GENIUS LOCI

The 'spirit' of a place. This can be affected by the people who live in the place; by ley line orientation (positive or negative); by events that occur in the place, such as murder or extreme suffering; and by other inputs of positive or negative influence.

GHOST HIGHWAY

A term for a 'green' energy line that is used to explain how ghost entities travel from one place to another, in the same way that we use roads; also known as ghost paths.

GHOSTPRINT

A handprint left in flour or dust by a spectre.

GHOST RESCUE

The work of psychics or mediums who apparently release entities from the ghost realm and help them reach the afterworld. Similar to exorcism, except that techniques used in ghost rescue are far gentler and some believe kinder, as ghost rescue takes into account the wishes and feelings of the ghost, whereas exorcism does not.

GHOSTSTEP

A footprint left in flour or dust by a spectre.

JINX FACTOR

Locations subject to the 'jinx factor' bring about camera malfunctions, video equipment jamming or inexplicable interference by supernatural agencies to reclaim photographic or video evidence of their existence. For example, a photograph of a ghost goes missing for no reason, a processed camera film is completely blank or a video tape of ghost phenomena wipes itself clean for no reason.

KHU

An ancient Egyptian word for a ghost.

LEY LINE

A straight line of aligned landmarks (such as tors, rocky outcrops and hills) occurring naturally in the landscape along which flows an unknown force, possibly related to electromagnetism. Ley lines occur naturally, but nearly always include additional sites built by man, such as castles or churches. These normally have spiritual or ritualistic importance and include megalithic monuments, burial mounds and historic buildings.

MANES
A general term used by the Romans to describe ghosts.

MATERIALISATION
A stage 4 manifestation that has enough energy to become physically real in the living world.

MEDIUM
Someone who is sensitive to ghosts and is unusually receptive to them. Some mediums relay messages supposedly from the other side, others use their power to aid psychic investigations. Most mediums have the ability to become temporarily possessed by a ghost and to allow the ghost to speak through them. The paranormal community is fraught with fake mediums, who prey on vulnerable people, so use caution before engaging their services.

ORB
A commonly used term for a stage 1 energy genesis.

OTHER SIDE
In many beliefs, the other side is the place where spirits go when the body dies. In broader terms, it is also used to describe a place where anything believed to remain after death exists. Also known as the afterworld.

OUIJA BOARD
A circular board with the letters of the alphabet on it that sometimes also contains key words, such as 'Yes' and 'No'. Ouija boards are used to contact the spirits of the dead, who supposedly spell out messages to the living by moving an upturned glass or planchette over the letters on the board. Ouija boards are often regarded as a children's game and indeed started out as a Victorian pastime. They should not, however, be taken lightly, as they can disturb the minds of sensitive individuals and some children. Ouija boards can also affect the genius loci of a place. The word 'ouija' comes from the French and German words for 'Yes' – 'Oui' and 'Ja'.

PARANORMAL INDUCTION
The introduction of a spirit entity to a new location by the spirit attaching itself to a person or persons and travelling with them to a new site.

PASSING CONDITIONS
Physical symptoms inflicted temporarily on a medium or psychic by a ghost entity. The conditions vary from case to case, but are normally connected with conditions experienced by the dead entity at their time of death. Passing conditions sometimes linger for a short while after the communication has ceased before fading away.

PINPOINT LIGHTS
Dots of light are often experienced at haunted locations. These are often recorded as being seen when a ghost is trying to manifest. The lights dart around in an apparently random manner and are normally azure blue or white in colour.

PSYCHIC EPICENTRE
The point where psychic energy is most highly focussed. This can be a room, an area or a physical object.

RADIOTELETHESIS
This is where a witness takes on the feelings of the ghost. This can be an emotion, a physical pain connected with the death of the ghost or the ghost's fear of the witness. It is different from clairsentience in that it is involuntary and uncontrolled.

SÉANCE
A controlled attempt to communicate with the dead, usually involving a group of people who concentrate in a combined effort.

SPIRIT EXTRA
The term used to describe ghosts in photographs – used in the Victorian era when fake ghost photography was at its peak.

TABLE TILTING
The inexplicable tilting of tables, apparently of their own accord, but believed to be a form of communication from the dead. Table tilting normally takes place during a séance.

TASH/THEVSHI
Irish words for ghosts.

TELLURIC ENERGY
Energy of an unknown origin, but believed to come from the Earth. Also known as 'free energy' and 'earth energy'. Telluric is a derivative of 'tellurian', meaning 'terrestrial'.

TELLURIC ENERGY FIELD

A point at which telluric energy gathers, such as ley-line convergence, a window area or a megalithic site (e.g. Stonehenge). A telluric energy field can span a large area from the energy centre (i.e. the standing stones, convergence point, etc.) and can be sensed by psychics at a considerable distance from the source.

TIMESLIP

A rip in the fabric of time whereby the past or future slips into the present and is experienced audibly, visually or sometimes physically, by people from the present. Timeslips often occur on or near ley lines.

TRIGGER PERSON

A person whose very presence can induce paranormal activity.

VIGIL

Another term for a ghost hunt or investigation.

WINDOW AREA

A location where the ether is such that it may be exploited by supernatural forces to a greater extent than in other areas. Window areas can be created by uncontrolled use of an ouija board, occult ritual or track magic and, in some cases, the confluence of two or more ley lines.

Buildings or locations on single ley lines can also become window areas if they are subjected to occult practices or extreme attention is drawn to them for their 'paranormal' interest. For example if lots of people come to a building to see and discuss ghosts, then the location itself becomes a magnet for ethereal presences and may become a window area.

Investigation Techniques

AUTOMATIC WRITING/SÉANCES

Attempts to 'talk' to ghosts are generally conducted via the Ouija Board but another method is 'the flying pencil' (as it was referred to in ancient China). In the west we call it 'automatic writing' and you need some psychic ability to develop this skill. Usually the psychic will sit down with a pencil and notebook, go into the trance state and eventually, after starting slowly, their pencil will 'fly' across the pages writing messages at great speed. Opinions are divided over what exactly is happening and if, indeed, the psychic is in communication with ghosts, it may be that the sitter is in touch with their spirit guides or even in touch with their own subconscious mind. Séances involve using a number of people to share their group energy to make contact with the dead. There is evidence that séances can and do work if there is a genuinely gifted medium leading the group as well as a spirit with an important message to communicate.

AUDIO RECORDING

Tape recorders or dictaphones serve several purposes; the primary function is to capture unexplained sounds and these are sometimes heard at the time of the investigation but can also often only be heard only at playback (EVPs), which is perhaps even more interesting! The secondary function is to record witness interviews and possible communications/séances.

BREEZE DETECTION

Candles can be useful for detecting unnatural breeze variations and sometimes spirits may make their presence known by elongating the flame, snuffing it out and/or relighting it. The use of candles must be carefully weighed against their potential as fire risks.

CHALK MARKING

This is useful and long-established method for detecting the anomalous movement of large objects or furniture. This has largely been superseded now by more sophisticated electronic tools, which are usually based on burglar alarm technology such as movement sensors and infrared proximity detectors.

DIODE RECORDING

Diodes are small gizmos that you can buy from specialist amateur radiobuilders' shops. Some paranormal investigators swear by the effectiveness of them for recording spirit voices. A diode functions as a very primitive radio receiver. It can't be tuned but it does produce high quality spirit voices. Attach it to a short (6–8 cm) aerial, then plug it into your recorder via a jack. Set recording sensitivity to its highest level and feel free to experiment with the length of the aerial.

DOWSING

As we have discovered at APIS, dowsing is an invaluable aid in the detection of lines of energy, commonly referred to as ley lines. These can provide us not only with evidence of whether or not a building is haunted, but also if it is, where the most likely haunting 'hot spots' are located.

ELECTROMAGNETIC FIELD MONITORING

Probably the single most useful piece of electronic hardware that you can take on a vigil is the EMF meter, used to detect unnatural variations in the electromagnetic field. These variations are associated with paranormal activity and their effectiveness was proven for us at the Blacksmith's Arms investigation ,where Andy Garrett's EMF meter, used immediately after the sighting of an apparition by the landlord, showed up a 'surge' in the electromagnetic field, which followed the path taken by the apparition! It should be remembered that there is a cheap alternative to the EMF meter – the compass. It will not give you as much information as an EMF meter but it is useful for magnetic field monitoring, and very strong electromagnetic variations can be detected by the wild swinging of the compass needle. They take up little room and are also useful for their normal use – determining directions at any location. I always carry one with me.

FLOUR DUSTING/MARKING

This method (flour dusting) may pick up 'ghostprints' – marks of hand and foot prints have been detected in this way (as at Michelham Priory in 1992). Flour marking of small objects is one way of detecting any anomalous movement of those objects.

HYPNOTISM

Hypnotising a member of the team who volunteers to be a 'channel' for communicating with the ghosts at a haunted location is a rarely used technique that should only be considered if there is a suitably qualified and experienced hypnotherapist on the investigation team.

INFRARED VIDEO RECORDING / VIDEO OBSERVATION

We now have 'see in the dark' video recorders at APIS, probably the greatest advance in paranormal investigation equipment in recent years. We are now able to capture orbs, streaks and pinpoints of light, which occur in total (or oLux) light conditions. Video cameras may also be adjusted for daylight settings to catch anomalous images on film and to record witness interviews, general location appearance and automatic writing/séances.

INTERVIEWS

A key part of the investigation (usually undertaken by the Team Leader) of staff, owners etc., concerning their own experiences or the experiences of others.

LOG BOOKS

From day one of our investigations APIS has put great reliance on recording any unusual occurrences with timed entries for members' comments.

MAPPING

A plan of the building that we are investigating is invaluable for several reasons. It can be remote-dowsed to detect the presence of 'green' energy lines and 'black streams'. It may be used to show the positions of various objects and furniture and as a general floor plan. The map may also be used to show where watch posts will be set up.

MUSIC

Playing music has been used effectively as a technique to encourage ghostly phenomena to happen at some vigils, it may be worth a try!

PHOTOGRAPHY

An essential element of any investigation; however, flash photography has to be controlled by the Team Leader. It may pay dividends to photograph the entire location before, during and after the vigil. APIS has achieved particularly interesting results after an investigation at Henrick's in Royston!

PSYCHICS/MEDIUMS

Almost all paranormal investigation groups use psychics on their investigations now. The drawback is that we are all using one unexplained phenomenon to explain another. The important thing is to give your medium no information about the haunting and the spiritual aspect is one that shouldn't be overlooked. Every bit of information given by the psychic(s) needs to be noted and every attempt should be made to verify this information later. When teamed up with a psychic member of APIS I like to record timed entries in the logbook about their impressions e.g. 'I feel a great sadness' or 'I feel frightened'. I strongly believe that this is just as worthy of being recorded as the temperature and humidity, sightings, sounds heard, smells noticed etc. because it is very real to the person concerned and it may be compared later with other impressions, received by other sensitives, at other times in the same locations. If we get matching sensations then that is particularly interesting!

REMOTE THERMAL SCANNING/TEMPERATURE & HUMIDITY MONITORING

A non-contact thermometer that measures temperature by firing a laser beam may find unseen presences and uncover cold spots. Temperature and humidity monitors have formed an essential part of APIS investigations from our first vigil onwards. The humidity meter is useful for ruling out ball lightning as a cause of possible paranormal effects, as it is known that ball lightning occurs at times of high humidity.

ROOM SEALING

Where there are areas of localised phenomena reported it may be prudent to seal the room/s with sticky tape and paper strips signed by the sealer (usually the Team Leader) and attached in such a way that any tampering by a human agency would be obvious. Particularly useful for trigger object experimentation.

'TRAPS'

Sugar has been used for centuries in ghost watching and it can be useful both to detect unexplained footsteps and to catch fraudsters. The other useful old standby when fraud is suspected is thin string or fishing line. Tying the thin line to a door, bed or any furniture suspected of being moved, which is tied loosely at the other end to the investigator's finger, can be extremely useful in such cases. It may also be tied across doorways when children are suspected of getting up in the night and causing mischief or if someone is sleepwalking.

TRIGGER OBJECTS

These are designed to attract the attention of ghosts and may take a variety of forms e.g. an open Bible, coins on paper outlined in pencil, pebbles in a tray of sand etc. They should be left alone by the investigation team, preferably in the sealed room(s).